Why Worry?

by George Lincoln Walton, M.D.

The legs of the stork are long, the legs of the duck are short; you cannot make the legs of the stork short, neither can you make the legs of the duck long. Why worry?--Chwang Tsze.

TO MY LONG-SUFFERING FAMILY AND CIRCLE OF FRIENDS, WHOSE PATIENCE HAS BEEN TRIED BY MY EFFORTS TO ELIMINATE WORRY, THIS BOOK IS AFFECTIONATELY DEDICATED.

PREFACE.

No apology is needed for adding another to the treatises on a subject whose importance is evidenced by the number already offered the public.

The habit of worry is not to be overcome by unaided resolution. It is hoped that the victim of this unfortunate tendency may find, among the homely illustrations and commonplace suggestions here offered, something to turn his mind into more healthy channels. It is not the aim of the writer to transform the busy man into a philosopher of the indolent and contemplative type, but rather to enable him to do his work more effectively by eliminating undue solicitude. This elimination is consistent even with the "strenuous life."

One writer has distinguished between normal and abnormal worry, and directed his efforts against the latter. Webster's definition of worry (A state of undue solicitude) obviates the necessity of deciding what degree and kind of worry is abnormal, and directs attention rather to deciding what degree of solicitude may be fairly adjudged undue.

In the treatment of a subject of this character a certain amount of repetition is unavoidable. But it is hoped that the reiteration of fundamental principles and of practical hints will aid in the application of the latter. The aim is the gradual establishment of a frame of mind. The reader who looks for the annihilation of individual worries, or who hopes to influence another by the direct application of the suggestions, may prepare, in the first instance for disappointment, in the second, for trouble.

The thanks of the writer are due to Miss Amy Morris Homans, Director of the Boston Normal School of Gymnastics, for requesting him to make to her students the address which forms the nucleus of these pages.

GEORGE L. WALTON.

BOSTON, April, 1908.

CONTENTS

DEFINITIONS.

WORRY. A state of undue solicitude.

HYPOCHONDRIA. A morbid mental condition characterized by undue solicitude regarding the health, and undue attention to matters thereto pertaining.

OBSESSION. An unduly insistent and compulsive thought, habit of mind, or tendency to action.

DOUBTING FOLLY (Folie du doute.) A state of mind characterized by a tendency unduly to question, argue and speculate upon ordinary matters.

NEURASTHENIA. A form of nervous disturbance characterized by exhaustion and irritability.

PHOBIA. An insistent and engrossing fear without adequate cause, as judged by ordinary standards.

OCCUPATION NEUROSIS. A nervous disorder in which pain, sometimes with weakness and cramp, results from continued use of a part.

PSYCHO-THERAPY. Treatment through the mind.

No other technical terms are used.

I.

INTRODUCTORY

When Thales was asked what was difficult he said, "To know oneself"; and what was easy, "To advise another."

Marcus Aurelius counselled, "Let another pray, 'Save Thou my child,' but do thou pray, 'Let me not fear to lose him.'"

Few of us are likely to attain this level; few, perhaps, aspire to do so. Nevertheless, the training which falls short of producing complete self-control may yet accomplish something in the way of fitting us, by taking the edge off our worry, to react more comfortably to our surroundings, thus not only rendering us more desirable companions, but contributing directly to our own health and happiness.

Under the ills produced by faulty mental tendencies I do not include cancer and the like. This inclusion seems to me as subversive of the laws of nature as the cure of such disease by mental treatment would be miraculous. At the same time, serious disorders surely result from faulty mental tendencies.

In this category we must include, for example, hypochondria, a disturbance shown by undue anxiety concerning one's own physical and mental condition. This disorder, with the allied fears resulting from the urgent desire to be always absolutely safe, absolutely well, and absolutely comfortable, is capable, in extreme cases, of so narrowing the circle of pleasure and of usefulness that the sufferer might almost as well have organic disease.

Neurasthenia (nervous prostration) has for its immediate exciting cause some overwork or stress of circumstance, but the sufferer not infrequently was already so far handicapped by regrets for the past, doubts for the present, and anxieties for the future, by attention to minute details and by unwillingness to delegate responsibilities to others, that he was exhausted by his own mental travail before commencing upon the overwork which precipitated his breakdown. In such cases the occasion of the collapse may have been his work, but the underlying cause was deeper. Many neurasthenics who think they are "all run down" are really "all wound up." They carry their stress with them.

Among the serious results of faulty mental habit must be included also the doubting folly (_folie du doute_). The victim of this disorder is so querulously anxious to make no mistake that he is forever returning to see if he has turned out the gas, locked the door, and the like; in extreme cases he finally doubts the actuality of his own sensations, and so far succumbs to chronic indecision as seriously to handicap his efforts. This condition has been aptly termed a "spasm of the attention."

The apprehensive and fretful may show, in varying degree, signs of either or all these conditions, according as circumstances may direct their attention.

Passing from serious disorders to minor sources of daily discomfort, there are few individuals so mentally gifted that they are impervious to the distress occasioned by variations of temperature and of weather; to the annoyance caused by criticism, neglect, and lack of appreciation on the part of their associates; to active resentment, even anger, upon moderate provocation; to loss of temper when exhausted; to embarrassment in unusual situations; to chronic indecision; to the sleeplessness resulting from mental preoccupation; and above all, to the futile regrets, the querulous doubts, and the undue anxiety included under the term _worry_, designated by a recent author "the disease of the age."

Something may be accomplished in the way of lessening all these ills by continuous, properly directed effort on the part of the individual. Every inroad upon one faulty habit strengthens the attack upon all, and each gain means a step toward the acquisition of a mental poise that shall give its possessor comparative immunity from the petty annoyances of daily life.

In modern psycho-therapy the _suggestion_, whether on the part of the physician or of the patient, plays a prominent part, and it is in this direction, aside from the advice regarding occupation and relaxation, that my propositions will trend. I shall not include, however, suggestions depending for their efficacy upon self-deceit, such as might spring, for example, from the proposition that if we think there is a fire in the stove it warms us, or that if we break a pane in the bookcase thinking it a window, we inhale with pleasure the resulting change of air. The suggestions are intended to appeal to the reason, rather than to the imagination.

The special aim will be to pay attention to the different varieties of worry, and to offer easily understood and commonplace suggestions which any one may practice daily and continuously, at last automatically, without interfering with his routine work or recreation. Indeed the tranquil mind aids, rather than hinders, efficient work, by enabling its possessor to pass from duty to duty without the hindrance of undue solicitude.

In advising the constitutional worrier the chief trouble the physician finds is an active opposition on the part of the patient. Instead of accepting another's estimate of his condition, and another's suggestions for its relief, he comes with a preconceived notion of his own difficulties, and with an insistent demand for their instant relief by drug or otherwise. He uses up his mental energy, and loses his temper, in the effort to convince his physician that he is not argumentative. In a less unreasonable, but equally difficult class, come those who recognize the likeness in the portrait painted by the consultant, but who say they have tried everything he suggests, but simply "can't."

It is my hope that some of the argumentative class may recognize, in my description, their own case instead of their neighbor's, and may of their own initiative adopt some of the suggestions; moreover, that some of the acquiescent, but despairing class will renew their efforts in a different spirit. The aim is, not to accomplish a complete and sudden cure, but to gain something every day, or if losing a little to-day, to gain a little to-morrow, and ultimately to find one's self on a somewhat higher plane, without discouragement though not completely freed from the trammels entailed by faulty mental habit.

II.

EPICURUS AS A MENTAL HEALER

'Tis to believe what men inspired of old, Faithful, and faithfully informed, unfold.

Cowper.

The suggestions offered in the following pages are not new. Many of them were voiced by Epicurus three hundred years before Christ, and even then were ancient history. Unfortunately Epicurus had his detractors. One, Timocrates, in particular, a renegade from his school, spread malicious and unfounded reports of his doings and sayings, reports too easily credited then, and starting, perhaps, the misconception which to-day prevails regarding the aims of this philosopher.

But when Marcus Aurelius, nearly five centuries later, decided to endow a philosophical professoriate he established the Epicurean as one of the four standard schools. The endorsement of such a one should surely predispose us to believe the authentic commentators of Epicurus, and to discredit the popular notion which makes his cult synonymous with the gratification of the appetites, instead of with the mental tranquility to which he regarded sensual pleasures so detrimental that he practically limited his diet, and that of his disciples, to bread and water.

It is of special encouragement to such of us as painfully realize our meagre equipment for reaching a high plane of self-control, to learn that Epicurus was by nature delicate and sensitive. At seven years of age, we are told, he could not support himself on tiptoe, and called himself the feeblest of boys. It is said that in his boyhood he had to be lifted from his chair, that he could not look on the sun or a fire, and that his skin was so tender as to prevent his wearing any dress beyond a simple tunic. These physical characteristics suggest the makings of a first class "fuss" and inveterate worrier. In this event his emancipation from such tendencies must have been due to the practice of his own philosophy.

As an antidote for the fear of death and the miraculous in the heavens Epicurus urges the study of Nature, showing his appreciation of the fact that one thought can only be driven out by another, as well as of the importance of the open air treatment of depressing fears.

That he recognized the doubting folly and its evils is shown by the following Maxim for the Wise man:

"He shall be steady in his opinion and not wavering and doubtful in everything."

To the hypochondriac he said:

"Health in the opinion of some is a precious thing; others rank it among the indifferent." Again:

"If the body be attacked by a violent pain the evil soon has an end; if, on the contrary, the pain be languishing and of long duration it is sensible beyond all doubt of some pleasure therefrom. Thus, most chronical distempers have intervals that afford us more satisfaction and ease than the distempers we labor under cause pain." And further:

"The Wise man takes care to preserve the unequivocable blessing of an undisturbed and quiet mind even amidst the groans and complaints which excess of pain extorts from him." He states, again, that one can be happy though blind.

Regarding insomnia, he recognized the futility of expecting restful sleep to follow a day of fret and worry. He says:

"He shall enjoy the same tranquility in his sleep as when awake."

Epicurus realized that the apparent inability of the old to acquire new habits is due rather to lack of attention, and to indifference or preoccupation, than to lack of aptitude. He placed, in fact, no limit to the age for learning new methods, stating in his letter to Meneceus,--

"Youth is no obstacle to the study of philosophy--neither ought we to be ashamed to concentrate our later years to the labor of speculation. Man has no time limit for learning, and ought never to want strength to cure his mind of all the evils that afflict it."

Epicurus does not counsel seclusion for the cultivation of tranquility, but holds that mental equipoise "may be maintained though one mingles with the world, provided he keeps within the bounds of temperance, and limits his desires to what is easily obtained."

Curiously enough, in view of the idea of epicureanism which has become proverbial, Epicurus regards the avoidance of excess a logical and necessary step toward the tranquil life, and among other admonitions is found the following Maxim:

"The Wise man ought never to drink to excess, neither must he spend the nights revelling and feasting."

We may conclude our selection from the Maxims of Epicurus by one which strikes a body-blow at worry and the allied faulty mental habits:

"That being who is happy and immortal is in no way solicitous or uneasy on any account, neither does he torment or tease others; anger is unworthy of his greatness ... for all these things are the property of weakness."

Such then, was the real Epicurus, not a seeker after effeminate luxury, but a chaste and frugal philosopher, serene of mien, and of gentle disposition, firm in his friendships, but sacrificing to them none of the high ideals which characterized his thought. He erred, doubtless, in the avoidance of responsibilities and in narrowing his efforts to promoting the happiness of his own immediate circle, but he was fearless in the defence of his principles and steadfast in the pursuit of the tranquility which for him included truth.

III.

MARCUS AURELIUS

Such a body of teachers distinguished by their acquirements and character will hardly be collected again; and as to the pupil, we have not had another like him since.

Long.

Marcus Aurelius Antoninus, the philosopher-Emperor, showed by practice as well as by precept that the tranquil mind is not incompatible with a life of action. Destined from birth to stand at the head of a great empire engaged in distant wars, threatened by barbaric invasion, and not without internal dissention, he was prepared not only to command armies but to govern himself. Fortunately we are not without a clue to his methods--he not only had the best of teachers, but continued his training all through his life. When we consider his labors, the claim of the busy man of to-day that he has "no time" seems almost frivolous.

The thoughts of Marcus Aurelius (of which the following citations are from Long's translation) were written, not for self exploration, nor from delight in rounded periods, but for his own guidance. That he was in fact guided by his principles no better illustration offers than his magnanimity toward the adherents of one who would have usurped the throne of the C鋥ars. The observation of Long that fine thoughts and moral dissertations from men who have not worked and suffered may be read, but will be forgotten, seems to have been exemplified in the comparative oblivion into which the philosophy of Epicurus has fallen.

It is with the ethical side of the philosophy of Marcus Aurelius that we are concerned, and with that portion only which bears on the question of mental equipoise.

"Begin the morning," he says, "by saying to thyself, I shall meet with the busybody, the ungrateful, arrogant, deceitful, envious, unsocial. All these things happen to them by reason of their ignorance of what is good and evil."

With regard to the habit of seclusion common among the self-conscious, he says:

"If thou didst ever see a hand cut off, or a foot, or a head, lying anywhere apart from the rest of the body, such does a man make himself, as far as he can, who is not content with what happens, and separates himself from others, or does any thing unsocial. Suppose that thou hast detached thyself from the natural unity--for thou wast made by nature a part, but now thou hast cut thyself off--yet here there is this beautiful provision, that it is in thy power again to unite thyself. God has allowed this to no other part, after it has been separated and cut asunder, to come together again. But consider the kindness by which he has distinguished man, for he has put it in his power not to be separated at all from the universal; and when he has been separated, he has allowed him to return and to resume his place as a part."

On the futile foreboding which plays so large a part in the tribulation of the worrier, he says:

"Do not disturb thyself by thinking of the whole of thy life. Let not thy thoughts at once embrace all the various troubles which thou mayest expect to befall thee; but on every occasion ask thyself, What is there in this which is intolerable and past bearing? for thou wilt be ashamed to confess. In the next place remember that neither the future nor the past pains thee, but only the present. But this is reduced to a very little, if thou only circumscribest it, and chidest thy mind, if it is unable to hold out against even this." Again: "Let not future things disturb thee, for thou wilt come to them, if it shall be necessary, having with thee the same reason which now thou usest for present things."

On the dismissal of useless fret, and concentration upon the work in hand, he says:

"Labor not as one who is wretched, nor yet as one who would be pitied or admired; but direct thy will to one thing only, to put thyself in motion and to check thyself, as the social reason requires."

Regarding senseless fears he counsels:

"What need is there of suspicious fear, since it is in thy power to inquire what ought to be done? And if thou seest clear, go by this way content, without turning back: but if thou dost not see clear, stop and take the best advisers. But if any other things oppose thee, go on according to thy powers with due consideration, keeping to that which appears to be just. For it is best to reach this object, and if thou dost fail, let thy failure be in attempting this. He who follows reason in all things is both tranquil and active at the same time, and also cheerful and collected."

On irritation at the conduct of others:

"When thou art offended with any man's shameless conduct, immediately ask thyself, Is it possible, then, that shameless men should not be in the world? It is not possible. Do not, then, require what is impossible. For this man also is one of those shameless men who must of necessity be in the world. Let the same considerations be present in thy mind in the case of the knave and the faithless man, and of every man who does wrong in any way."

Regarding the hypochondriacal tendency he reverts to Epicurus, thus:

"Epicurus says, In my sickness my conversation was not about my bodily sufferings, nor did I talk on such subjects to those who visited me; but I continued to discourse on the nature of things as before, keeping to this main point, how the mind, while participating in such movements as go on in the poor flesh, shall be free from perturbations and maintain its proper good.... Do, then, the same that he did both in sickness, if thou art sick, and in any other circumstances;... but to be intent only on that which thou art now doing and on the instrument by which thou doest it."

These quotations will serve to show the trend of the reflections of this remarkable man. After reviewing this epitome of ethical philosophy I might stop and counsel the worrier to study the thoughts of Marcus Aurelius and other philosophers, whose practical suggestions are similar, notwithstanding their diversity of views regarding the ultimate object of the training. I shall venture, however, to elaborate the subject from the present view-point, even though the principles of Marcus Aurelius are as applicable now as they were in the days of the Roman Empire.

No reminder is needed of the wealth and efficacy of suggestion in the Book which contains the statement that "the Kingdom of God is within you," and that "A merry heart doeth good like a medicine; but a broken spirit drieth the bones." One of its suggestions was paralleled by the philosopher-poet when he wrote:

"Latius regnes avidum domando Spiritum, quam si Libyam remotis Gadibus iungas et uterque Poenus Serviat uni."

IV.

ANALYSIS OF WORRY

Of these points the principal and most urgent is that which reaches the passions; for passion is produced no otherwise than by a disappointment of one's desires and an incurring of one's aversions. It is this which introduces perturbations, tumults, misfortunes, and calamities; this is the spring of sorrow, lamentation and envy; this renders us envious and emulous, and incapable of hearing reason.

Epictetus.

Under this rather pretentious title an attempt is made to indicate certain elements of worry. No claim is made that the treatment of the subject is exhaustive.

The motto "Don't Worry" has inspired many homilies. But the mere resolve to follow this guide to happiness will no more instantaneously free one from the meshes of worry than the resolve to perform a difficult gymnastic feat will insure its immediate accomplishment.

The evils of worry as well as of its frequent associate, anger, have been dwelt upon by writers philosophical, religious, and medical. "Worry," says one author, "is the root of all cowardly passions,--jealousy, fear, the belittling of self, and all the introspective forms of depression are the children of worry." The symptoms and the evil results seem to receive more elaborate and detailed attention than the treatment. "Eliminate it," counsels this writer; "Don't worry," advises another. "Such advice is superficial," says their critic, "it can only be subdued by our ascending into a higher atmosphere, where we are able to look down and comprehend the just proportions of life." "Cultivate a quiet and peaceful frame of mind," urges another; and still another advises us to "occupy the mind with better things, and the best--is a habit of confidence and repose."

From such counsel the average individual succeeds in extracting nothing tangible. The last writer of those I have quoted comes perhaps the nearest to something definite in directing us to occupy the mind with better things; in the suggestions I have to offer the important feature is the effort to replace one thought by another, though not necessarily by a better one. If we succeed in doing this, we are making a step toward acquiring the habit of confidence and repose.

The simple admonition not to worry is like advising one not to walk awkwardly who has never learned to walk otherwise. If we can find some of the simpler elements out of which worry is constructed, and can learn to direct our attack against these, the proposition "Don't worry" will begin to assume a tangible form.

We can at least go back one step, and realize that it is by way of the unduly insistent thought that most of these faulty mental habits become established. It might be claimed that fear deserves first mention, but the insistent thought in a way includes fear, and in many cases is independent of it.

The insistent thought magnifies by concentration of attention, and by repetition, the origin of the worry. If my thoughts dwell on my desire for an automobile this subject finally excludes all others, and the automobile becomes, for the time being, the most important thing in the world, hence I worry. Into this worry comes no suggestion of fear--this emotion would be more appropriate, perhaps, if I acquired the automobile and attempted to run it. If, now, I have trained myself to concentrate my attention elsewhere before such thoughts become coercive, the automobile quickly assumes its proper relation to other things, and there is no occasion for worry. This habit of mind once acquired regarding the unessentials of life, it is remarkable how quickly it adapts itself to really important matters.

Take a somewhat more serious question. I fear I may make a blunder. If I harbor the thought, my mind is so filled with the disastrous consequences of the possible blunder that I finally either abandon the undertaking or approach it with a trepidation that invites failure. If, on the other hand, I have learned to say that even if I make a blunder it will only add to my experience, then apply myself whole-minded to the task, I have made a direct attack on worry.

The qualification unduly is not to be forgotten; a certain discrimination must be exercised before entirely condemning the insistent thought. The insistent thought that one's family must be fed is not a morbid sign. In fact, he also errs who can eliminate this thought and enjoy the ball game. It is not for the deviate of this type that I am writing. Nevertheless, the over-solicitous victim of the "New England Conscience" can almost afford to take a few lessons from the ne'er-do-weel.

The practical bearing of this attempt to analyze worry is obvious. If it is through the insistent desire for an automobile that I worry, I must bring my training to bear, not on the worry, which is elusive, but on the desire, which is definite. I must fortify myself with what philosophy I can acquire, and must console myself with such compensations as my situation may offer; and above all, I must _get busy_, and occupy hands and brain with something else. If, on my travels, I worry over the sluggish movement of the train, it is because of the insistent thought that I must arrive on time. In this event I should practice subduing the insistent thought, rather than vaguely direct my efforts against the worry. In the majority of cases I can bring myself to realize that the question of my arrival is not vital. Even in case I am missing an important engagement I may modify the dominance of the thought by reflecting that I cannot expect to be wholly immune from the misfortunes of mankind; it is due me, at least once in a lifetime, to miss an important engagement,--why fret because this happens to be the appointed time? Why not occupy my thoughts more profitably than in rehearsing the varied features of this unavoidable annoyance?

If we fret about the weather it is because of an insistent desire that the weather shall conform to our idea of its seasonableness. If we complain of the chill of May it is not because the cold is really unbearable, but because we wonder if spring will ever come. If we fume on a hot day in July it is because the weather is altogether too seasonable to suit us.

We spend far too much thought on the weather, a subject that really deserves little attention except by those whose livelihood and safety depend upon it. Suppose a runaway passes the window at which we are sitting, with collar off, handkerchief to our heated brow, squirming to escape our moist and clinging garments, and being generally miserable. We rush out of doors to watch his course, and for the next few minutes we do not know whether it is hot or cold, perspiring less during our exertions, I strongly suspect, than we did while sitting in the chair. At all events, it is obvious that our thoughts played quite as great a part in our discomfort as did the heat of the day.

Suppose now, instead of devoting all our attention to the weather we should reason somewhat as follows:

As long as I live on this particular planet, I shall be subject perhaps three days out of four, to atmospheric conditions which do not suit me. Is it worth my while to fret during those three days and to make it up by being elated on the fourth? Why not occupy myself with something else and leave the weather for those who have no other resource? Or, as someone has said, why not "make friends with the weather?" If one will cultivate this frame of mind he will be surprised to find that a certain physical relief will follow. In the first place, he will lessen the excessive perspiration which is the invariable accompaniment of fret, and which in its turn produces more discomfort than the heat itself.

We have selected, so far, the comparatively unimportant sources of mental discomfort, fret, and worry. The reader who can truthfully say that such annoyances play no part in his mental tribulations may pass them and accept congratulations. The reader who cannot be thus congratulated, but who is impatient to attack the major sources of worry, must be reminded at this point that he must practice on the little worries before he can accomplish anything with the great. The method is the same. The philosophy that will make us content with the weather will do something toward establishing the mental poise which shall enable us to withstand with comparative equanimity the most tragic of misfortunes that may fall to our lot.

To draw an example from the more serious disorders, let us consider the hypochondriac, who harbors the insistent thought that he must be always perfectly well, that each of his sensations must conform to his ideal, and that each function must follow regulations imposed by himself. If he can learn to ignore this thought by realizing that an acute illness is preferable to life-long mental captivity; if he can learn to do what others do, and to concentrate his energies on outside affairs which shall displace the question of health; if he can learn to say "What I am doing is more important than how I am _feeling_;" he will have cured his hypochondria.

In the foundation of the structure we are studying is found _exaggerated self-consciousness_. Whatever is said, done, or left undone, by others is analyzed by the worrier with reference to its bearing on himself. If others are indifferent it depresses him, if they appear interested they have an ulterior motive, if they look serious he must have displeased them, if they smile it is because he is ridiculous. That they are thinking of their own affairs is the last thought to enter his mind.

I suppose it would be an affectation for any of us to deny that, as far as we are concerned, we are the centre of the universe. This conceit does us no harm so long as we remember that there are as many centres of the universe as there are people, cats, mice and other thinking animals. When we forget this our troubles begin. If I enter a strange shop and find they desire security, need I take this as a reflection on my credit? Need I expect to be invited to every entertainment I should like to attend, and to be excused from those that bore me, and shall I make no allowance for the attitude of my host? Is it not rather egotistic for me to suppose that others are vitally interested in the fact that I blush, tremble, or am awkward? Why then should I allow my conduct to be influenced by such trivial matters?

The order of training is, then, generally, to modify our self-consciousness by externalizing our thoughts and broadening our interests; specifically, to eliminate the unduly insistent habit of thought.

This analysis of worry and allied mental states may facilitate such training, but the practical value of the suggestions does not depend upon the acceptance of these theoretical considerations.

V.

WORRY AND OBSESSION

So much are men enured in their miserable estate, that no condition is so poore, but they will accept; so they may continue in the same.

Florio's Montaigne.

"You may as well be eaten by the fishes as by the worms," said the daughter of a naval commander to me one day, when discussing the perils of the sea. Such philosophy, applied to each of the vexatious and dangerous situations of daily life, would go far toward casting out worry.

We have already referred to two important elements at the foundation, and in the framework, of the elaborate superstructures we rear with such material as worry, doubts, fears and scruples. The first is _exaggerated self-consciousness_, the second the tendency to succumb to the compelling thought or impulse, technically termed obsession.

With regard to self-consciousness, the worrier will generally realize that even as a child he was exceptionally sensitive to criticism, censure, ridicule and neglect. He was prone to brood over his wrongs, to play the martyr, and to suffer with peculiar keenness the "slings and arrows of outrageous fortune." I remember once leaving the table on account of some censure or careless remark. I fancied I had thrown the whole family into a panic of contrition. On the first opportunity, I asked what they had said about it, and was told that they had apparently not noticed my departure. This salutary lesson prevented repetition of the act.

To the self-conscious person the mere entrance into a public vehicle may prove an ordeal. It is hard for him to realize that the general gaze has no peculiar relation to himself, and that if the gaze is prolonged this is due to no peculiarity of his beyond the blush or the trepidation that betrays his feeling. If he can acquire indifference to this feature of his case, through the reflection that to others it is only a passing incident, the blush and the trepidation will promptly disappear, and a step will have been taken towards gaining the self-control for which he aims.

The usual cause of stage-fright is exaggerated self-consciousness. The sufferer from stage-fright can hardly fail to be a worrier. A certain shyness, it would seem, may also result from too acute a consciousness of one's audience, as in the case of Tennyson, whom Benson quotes thus:

"I am never the least shy before great men. Each of them has a personality for which he or she is responsible; but before a crowd which consists of many personalities, of which I know nothing, I am infinitely shy. The great orator cares nothing about all this. I think of the good man, and the bad man, and the mad man, that may be among them, and can say nothing. He takes them all as one man. He sways them as one man."

This, I take it, hardly spelled stage-fright. At the same time, it is improbable that one so sensitive to criticism meant to convey the impression that it was of his audience alone he thought in shrinking from the effort.

It appears that Washington Irving suffered from actual stage-fright.

In the Library edition of Irving's works appears the following anecdote from the reminiscences of Mrs. Julia Ward Howe, then a young woman of twenty-three:

"I was present, with other ladies, at a public dinner given in honor of Charles Dickens by prominent citizens of New York. The ladies were not bidden to the feast, but were allowed to occupy a small ante-room which, through an open door, commanded a view of the tables. When the speaking was about to begin, a message came suggesting that we take possession of some vacant seats at the great table. This we were glad to do. Washington Irving was president of the evening, and upon him devolved the duty of inaugurating the proceedings by an address of welcome to the distinguished guest. People who sat near me whispered, 'He'll break down,--he always does.' Mr. Irving rose and uttered a sentence or two. His friends interrupted him by applause, which was intended to encourage him, but which entirely overthrew his self-possession. He hesitated, stammered, and sat down, saying, 'I cannot go on.'"

Cavendish, the chemist, suffered from a constitutional shyness attributable only to self-consciousness. He is said to have carried so far his aversion to contact with others, outside of his colleagues, that his dinner was always ordered by means of a note, and instant dismissal awaited the female domestic who should venture within his range of vision.

Lombroso cites, among his "Men of Genius," quite a list--Corneille, Descartes, Virgil, Addison, La Fontaine, Dryden, Manzoni, and Newton--of those who could not express themselves in public. Whatever part self-consciousness played in the individual case, we must class the peculiarity among the defects, not signs, of genius. "A tender heel makes no man an Achilles."

To the second faulty habit, obsession, I wish to devote special attention. This word we have already defined as an unduly insistent and compulsive thought, habit of mind, or tendency to action. The person so burdened is said to be obsessed.

Few children are quite free from obsession. Some must step on stones;

others must walk on, or avoid, cracks; some must ascend the stairs with the right foot first; many must kick posts or touch objects a certain number of times. Some must count the windows, pictures, and figures on the wallpaper; some must bite the nails or pull the eye-winkers. Consider the nail-biter. It cannot be said that he toils not, but to what end? Merely to gratify an obsession. He nibbles a little here and a little there, he frowns, elevates his elbow, and inverts his finger to reach an otherwise inaccessible corner. Does he enjoy it? No, not exactly; but he would be miserable if he discontinued.

An unusual, but characteristic obsession is told by a lady in describing her own childhood. She thought that on retiring she must touch nothing with her hands, after she had washed them, until she touched the inside of the sheets. In case she failed she must return and wash the hands again. The resulting manoeuvres are still fresh in her mind, particularly when her sister had preceded her to bed and she had to climb the footboard.

It is during childhood that we form most of the automatic habits which are to save time and thought in later life, and it is not surprising that some foolish habits creep in. As a rule, children drop these tendencies at need, just as they drop the roles assumed in play, though they are sometimes so absorbing as to cause inconvenience. An interesting instance was that of the boy who had to touch every one wearing anything red. On one occasion his whole family lost their train because of the prevalence of this color among those waiting in the station.

The longer these tendencies are retained in adult life, the greater the danger of their becoming coercive; and so far as the well-established case is concerned the obsessive act must be performed, though the business, social, and political world should come to a stand-still. Among the stories told in illustration of compulsive tendency in the great, may be instanced the touching of posts, and the placing of a certain foot first, in the case of Dr. Johnson, who, it appears, would actually retrace his steps and repeat the act which failed to satisfy his requirements, with the air of one with something off his mind.

A child who must kick posts is father to the man who cannot eat an egg which has been boiled either more or less than four minutes; who cannot work without absolute silence; who cannot sleep if steam-pipes crackle; and who must straighten out all the tangles of his life, past, present, and future, before he can close his eyes in slumber or take a vacation. The boy Carlyle, proud, shy, sensitive, and pugnacious, was father to the man who made war upon the neighbor's poultry, and had a room, proof against sound, specially constructed for his literary labors.

The passive obsessions are peculiarly provocative of worry. Such are extreme aversions to certain animals, foods, smells, sounds, and sights, or insistent discomfort if affairs are not ordered to our liking. A gentleman once told me that at the concert he did not mind if his neighbor followed the score, but when he consulted his programme during the performance it distressed him greatly.

Such instances illustrate the fact that when our obsessions rule us it is not the noise or the sight, but our idea of the fitness of things, that determines the degree of our annoyance. A person who cannot endure the crackling of the steam-pipe can listen with pleasure to the crackling of an open fire or the noise of a running brook.

It is said that the sensitive and emotional Erasmus had so delicate a digestion that he could neither eat fish nor endure the smell of it; but we are led to suspect that obsession played a part in his troubles when we further learn that he could not bear an iron stove in the room in which he worked, but had to have either a porcelain stove or an open fire.

If we can trust the sources from which Charles Reade drew his deductions regarding the character of the parental stock, Erasmus came fairly by his sensitive disposition. In "The Cloister and the Hearth" we find the father of Erasmus, fleeing from his native land, in fear of his life on account of a crime he thought he had committed, frozen, famished and exhausted, unable to enter the door of a friendly inn on account of his aversion to the issuing odors. Forced by his sufferings at last to enter the inn, he visits each corner in turn, analyzing its peculiar smell and choosing finally the one which seems to him the least obnoxious.

I have heard somewhere, but cannot place, the story of a prominent writer who was so disturbed by the mechanical lawn-mower of his neighbor that he insisted upon the privilege of defraying the expense of its replacement by the scythe.

Peculiar sensitiveness to sights, sounds and smells seems to be a common attribute of genius. This sort of sensitiveness has even been credited with being the main-spring of genius, but it is improbable that the curbing of such aversions would in any way endanger it. However this may be, such supersensitiveness ill becomes the rest of us, and these extreme aversions surely clog, rather than accelerate, our efforts.

* * * * *

The natural tendency of the healthy mind is to accustom itself to new sensations, as the ring on the finger, or the spectacles on the nose. The obsessive individual resists this tendency; he starts with the fixed idea that he cannot stand the annoyance, his resentment increases, and his sensations become more, instead of less, acute. His reaction to criticism, slight, and ridicule is similar; he is prepared to start, blush, and show anger on moderate provocation, and can often reproduce both the sensation and its accompanying physical signs by merely recalling the circumstance.

The passive as well as the active obsessions can be overcome by cultivating the commonplace, or average normal, attitude, and resolving gradually to accustom one's self to the disagreeable. This change of attitude can be made in adult life as well as in youth. "You cannot teach an old dog new tricks," we are told. The reason is not that the old dog cannot learn them, but that he does not want to. I met in Germany a British matron who was obsessed with the belief that she could not learn the language. At the end of four years' sojourn she entered a store and asked the price of an article.

"Four marks," was the answer.

"How much in English money?" she inquired.

"Why, madam, a mark is the same as a shilling."

"I don't know anything about that; how much is it in English?"

"Four shillings."

"Ah, quite so; you might have told me at once."

Experience has shown that no time in life precludes the acquirement of new knowledge and new habits by one who thinks it worth while to make the attempt. The elderly person will be surprised at his progress if he will bring to bear upon a new subject a mind free from doubts of its usefulness, doubts of his own ability, worry lest he is wasting valuable time, regrets for the past and plans for the future.

It is not always possible to say just where useful habit merges into obsession. A certain individual, we will say, invariably puts on the left shoe before the right. This is a useful habit, fixed by constant repetition, useful because it relieves the brain of conscious effort. But suppose he decides some morning to put on the right shoe before the left; this new order so offends his sense of the fitness of things that he finds it hard to proceed; if he perseveres, his feet feel wrong to him; the discomfort grows until finally he is impelled to remove the shoes and replace them in the usual order. In this case an act which started as a useful habit has been replaced by an obsession.

Suppose, again, a person obsessed by the fear of poison is prevented from washing his hands before eating. He sits down, perhaps, fully intending to proceed as if nothing had happened, but the thought occurs to him that he may have touched something poisonous, though his reason tells him this is most improbable. He reviews the events of the day and can find no suggestion of poison; still the thought of poison obtrudes itself, and he finds it impossible to put anything which he touches into his mouth. He next wonders if he has not already put something into his mouth. This thought produces a mental panic, the blood mounts to his head, he becomes incapable of coherent thought or speech, and the task of finishing his dinner would now be beyond his power even if he had not lost all taste for it.

Such illustrations of obsession in daily life, by no means rare, could be multiplied indefinitely, and may be perhaps better appreciated than the text-book illustration of the man who neglected to flick off with his whip a certain stone from the top of a wall, and who could not sleep until he had returned to the spot and performed the act.

Suppose a man has always worn high boots and is accustomed to a feeling of warmth about the ankles. The desire for warm ankles may finally so dominate him that he not only cannot wear low shoes in mid-summer, but he cannot wear slippers, even in a warm room; and finally, perhaps, finds that he must wear woollen socks to bed. By this time the desire for a certain sensation is in a fair way to become an obsession. When you assure him that many wear low shoes throughout the winter, he asks if their ankles really feel warm. That is not the question. The question is, can one accustom himself to the ankles feeling cool, just as he accustoms himself to his face feeling cool. If he can, he has conquered a sensory obsession, and has made a step toward fitting himself to meet more serious vicissitudes with equanimity.

Similar instances can be adduced in all realms of sensation, both general and special. One person cannot bear the light, and wears blue glasses; another cannot breathe out-door air, and wears a respirator; another cannot bear to see a person rock or to hear a person drum.

If a family or circle of friends is so constituted that some are obsessed to do certain things and others are obsessed not to stand them the foundation is laid for a degree of irritability inconsistent with mental health. Mrs. X. simply cannot stand hearing Mr. X. tap the floor, and if he continues, her discomfort becomes acute; the sound so dominates her that she can think of nothing else and can accomplish nothing until the sound is stopped. She can stand anything but that. The daughter, Miss X., hardly hears the tapping, and is irritated and impatient to the last degree on account of her mother's "silly" notion. What Miss X. simply cannot bear is hearing her brother continually clear his throat, and if he does not stop she must leave the room or "go wild." Unfortunately, meantime, Mr. X. is so obsessed to tap the floor that he cannot follow his task without it, and Master X. must clear his throat every few moments with a peculiar note because he "has catarrh."

Here we have a common starting-point for family discomfort, and here we have a clue to the advice of the physician who advises isolation as a step toward the cure of the member of the family who first breaks down, not simply under the stress of occupation, but of occupation plus the wear and tear of minor but constant sources of irritation.

* * * * *

It is said that the victim of jiu jitsu, by breaking one hold, places himself in the greater danger from the next. Similarly, after having conquered a few obsessions, one is overwhelmed with the obsession to set every one straight. Soukanhoff was right in warning the obsessive to beware of pedantry.

The question here presents itself whether this line of thought does not foster, rather than lessen, the pedantry and the self-study which it is intended to combat. Why not simply drop the worry and the doubt without further argument? The difficulty is that the mental processes of the over-scrupulous person are such that he cannot summarily drop a habit of thought. He must reason himself out of it. There is no limit to his ability if properly directed; he can gradually modify all his faulty tendencies, and may even finally acquire the habit of automatically dismissing worry, but it would be too much to expect that he suddenly change his very nature at command.

Soukanhoff's description of obsessives is peculiarly apt: "over-scrupulous, disquieted over trifles, indecisive in action, and anxious about their affairs. They are given early to morbid introspection, and are easily worried about their own indispositions or the illnesses of their friends. They are often timorous and apprehensive, and prone to pedantism. The moral sentiments are pronounced in most cases, and if they are, as a rule, somewhat exigent and egotistic, they have a lively sense of their own defects."

A common obsession is the compulsion to dwell upon the past, to reproduce the circumstances, and painfully to retrace the steps which we took in coming to an erroneous decision which led to a foolish, unnecessary, or perhaps even a wrong decision. One of my earliest impressions in golf was the remark of a veteran who was good enough to make a round with me. "If I had only approached better, I should have made that hole in five," I remarked, after taking seven strokes for a hole.

"Perhaps not," he replied; "if you had _approached better_, perhaps you would have putted worse and taken eight strokes for the hole. At all events, that hole is ancient history now, and you will play this one better if you leave that one alone."

He little realized how many times his advice would recur to me elsewhere than on the links. Retrospective worry can be absolutely eliminated from the most obsessive mind by the practice of the veteran's philosophy.

Mercier says the greatest intellectual gift is the ability to forget.

The conscientious self-analyst spends too much time in weighing his ability or inability to perform some task. Between his fear, his worry over the past, and his indecision whether the task should be attempted, he starts with an overwhelming handicap. If he learns to say, "Other people fail; it will not matter if I do this time," he will find the task already half accomplished.

The Rev. Francis Tiffany has observed that if a ship could think, and should imagine itself submerged by all the waves between here and Europe, it would dread to leave its moorings; but in reality it has to meet but one wave at a time.

The tendency of the average American in this bustling age, whether he is obsessive or not, is to live at least several hours in advance. On the train he takes no comfort and makes no observations, for his mind is upon his destination rather than on his journey.

* * * * *

Though the immediate object of these chapters is the promotion of the mental, and indirectly the physical, health of the individual, I cannot forbear referring to the effect of this training on the position of the individual in society and his relation toward his surroundings.

The endeavor to overcome obsessions is likely to be ignored by two classes: the self-centered individuals who see no reason for learning what they do not want to learn, and the individuals who have no time for, or interest in, self-training because of absorption in subjects of wider relation, as art, or science, or reform. The philosophy of Haeckel applies to both:

"Man belongs to the social vertebrates, and has, therefore, like all social animals, two sets of duties--first to himself, and secondly to the society to which he belongs. The former are the behests of self-love, or egoism, the latter love for one's fellows, or altruism. The two sets of precepts are equally just, equally natural, and equally indispensable. If a man desires to have the advantage of living in an organized community, he has to consult not only his own fortune, but also that of the society, and of the 'neighbors' who form the society. He must realize that its prosperity is his own prosperity, and that it cannot suffer without his own injury."

The individual who is ruled by his obsessions not only paves the way for needless and ultimate breakdown, but is in danger of gradually narrowing his field of usefulness and pleasure until he is in little better case than Simeon Stylites, who spent nearly half a century on the top of a monument. Nor has he even Simeon's consolation that he could come down if he chose; for it seems that the authorities sent messengers demanding his return, with orders to let him stay if he showed willingness to come down--and he stayed.

VI.

THE DOUBTING FOLLY

Jatgeir. I needed sorrow; others there may be who need faith, or joy--or doubt--

King Skule. Doubt as well?

Jatgeir. Ay; but then must the doubter be strong and sound.

King Skule. And whom call you the unsound doubter?

Jatgeir. He who doubts of his own doubt.

King Skule (slowly). That methinks were death.

Jatgeir. 'T is worse; 't is neither day nor night.

King Skule (quickly, as if shaking off his thoughts). Where are my weapons? I will fight and act, not think.

IBSEN: _The Pretenders_, Act iv.

A gentleman once told me that he rarely passed another in the street without wondering if he had not accosted him in an improper manner. He knew very well that he had not, but the more he dwelt upon the possibility, the more doubtful he became, until the impulse to settle the question became so strong that he would retrace his steps and inquire. He asked if nux vomica would help this trouble! I told him he needed mental training.

"I have tried that," he answered. "I keep saying to myself, 'I will not think of it,' but it is no use; my head becomes hot, my sight blurred, my thoughts confused, and the only relief I find is to settle the question."

I tried to point out the direction in which he was tending, and told him he must remind himself that even if he had accosted another improperly, it was a trifling matter compared to the injury to himself of giving way to this compulsion; moreover, the impression he would make upon the other by going back would be even worse than that of having so accosted him; and, finally, he must dwell upon the probability that he had not offended the man, instead of the possibility that he had. Having pursued this line of thought, he must force himself to think of something else until the besetting impulse was obliterated. I suggested that if a baseball player should become incapacitated for the game, he would not lessen his disappointment by reiterating, "I will not think of baseball," but if he persistently turned his thoughts and his practice to billiards he might in time forget baseball.

"I never played baseball," he replied, "and don't even know the rules."

This represents an extreme case of "doubting folly" a case in which the victim could no longer concentrate his thoughts on the simplest proposition outside the narrow circle to which his doubts had restricted him.

If we once allow ourselves to wonder whether we have turned off the water, enclosed the check, or mailed the letter, it is but a step to an uncomfortable frame of mind which can be relieved only by investigating the matter. This compulsion once acceded to, it becomes more and more easy to succumb. The next step is to blur, by constant repetition, the mental image of the act. In extreme cases the doubter, after turning the gas on and off a dozen times, is finally in doubt whether he can trust his own senses. A certain officer in a bank never succeeded in reaching home after closing hours without returning to try the door of the bank. Upon finding it locked, he would unlock it and disappear within, to open the vault, inspect the securities, and lock them up again. I once saw a victim of this form of doubt spend at least ten minutes in writing a check, and ten minutes more inspecting it, and, after all, he had spelled his own name wrong!

Constant supervision only impairs acts which should have become automatic. We have all heard of the centipede who could no longer proceed upon his journey when it occurred to him to question which foot he should next advance.

To other doubts are often added the doubt of one's own mental balance; but it is a long step from these faulty habits of mind to real mental unbalance, which involves an inability to plan and carry out a line of conduct consistent with one's station.

It took a young man at least fifteen minutes, in my presence, to button his waistcoat. He felt the lower button to reassure himself, then proceeded to the next. He then returned to the lower one, either distrusting his previous observation, or fearing it had become unbuttoned. He then held the lower two with one hand while he buttoned the third with the other. When this point was reached he called his sight to the aid of his feeling, and glued his eyes to the lower while he buttoned the upper, unbuttoning many meantime, to assure himself that he had buttoned them. This young man said he would sometimes stop on his way to the store in doubt whether he was on the right street, a doubt not quieted either by reading the sign or by asking a stranger, because the doubt would obtrude itself whether he could trust his sight and his hearing, indeed, whether he was really there or dreaming. Even this victim of extreme doubting folly conducted his business successfully so long as I knew him, and so comported himself in general as to attract no further comment than that he was "fussy."

These doubts lead to chronic indecision. How often, in deciding which of two tasks to take up, we waste the time which would have sufficed for the accomplishment of one, if not both.

The doubt and the indecision result directly from over-conscientiousness. It is because of an undue anxiety to do the right thing, even in trivial matters, that the doubter ponders indefinitely over the proper sequence of two equally important (or unimportant) tasks. In the majority of instances it is the right thing for him to pounce upon either. If he pounces upon the wrong one, and completes it without misgiving, he has at least accomplished something in the way of mental training. The chances are, moreover, that the harm done by doing the wrong thing first was not to be compared to the harm of giving way to his doubt, and either drifting into a state of ineffective revery or fretting himself into a frenzy of anxious uncertainty.

A gentleman once told me that after mailing a letter he would often linger about the box until the postman arrived, and ask permission to inspect his letter, ostensibly to see if he had put on the stamp, but in fact to reassure himself that he had really mailed the missive, although he knew perfectly well that he had done so. The life of the chronic doubter is full of these small deceits, though in most matters such persons are exceptionally conscientious.

This form of over-solicitude is peculiarly liable to attack those in whose hands are important affairs affecting the finances, the lives, or the health of others. I have known more than one case of the abandonment of a chosen occupation on account of the constant anxiety entailed by doubts of this nature. Nor are these doubts limited to the question whether one has done or left undone some particular act. An equally insistent doubt is that regarding one's general fitness for the undertaking. The doubter may spend upon this question more time than it would take to acquire the needed facility and experience.

Some one has said there are two things that no one should worry about: first, the thing that can't be helped; second, the thing that can. This is peculiarly true of the former.

Reflection upon the past is wise; solicitude concerning it is an anachronism. Suppose one has accepted a certain position and finds himself in doubt of his fitness for that position. Nothing can be more important than for him to decide upon his next line of conduct. Shall he resign or continue? Is he fit for the position, or, if not, can he acquire the fitness without detriment to the office? These are legitimate doubts. But the doubter who finds himself in this predicament adds to these legitimate doubts the question, "Ought I to have accepted the office?" This is the doubt he must learn to eliminate. He must remind himself that he has accepted the position, whether rightly or wrongly, and that the acceptance is ancient history. The question what shall he do next is sufficiently weighty to occupy all his attention without loading his mind with anxious doubts regarding the irrevocable past.

Suppose, in fact, the doubter has made a mistake; how shall he banish the worry? By reminding himself that others have made mistakes, why should not he, and that it is somewhat egotistic on his part to insist that, whatever others may do, he must do everything right. If this line of reasoning fails to console him, let him think of the greater mistakes he might have made. A financial magnate was once asked how he succeeded in keeping his mind free from worry. He replied, by contemplating the two worst things that could happen to him: losing all his property and going to jail. He had learned the lesson that one thought can be driven out only by another.

With regard to immediate doubts. If the over-scrupulous business or professional man, worn out after an exacting day's work, will stop and reflect, he will realize that much of his exhaustion is due to his having filled the day with such doubts as whether he is doing the wrong thing, or the right thing at the wrong time, whether he or someone else will miss an appointment or fail to meet obligations, and whether he or his assistants may make blunders.

Let him resolve some morning that he will proceed that day from task to task without allowing such thoughts to intrude. If he does so he will find that he has succeeded in his work at least as well as usual, and that he is comparatively fresh in the evening.

Why not try this every day?

* * * * *

So far we have only considered the most obvious and simple among the evidences of doubting folly. A still more obstinate tendency of the doubter is the insistent habit interminably to argue over the simplest proposition, particularly regarding matters pertaining to the health, comfort, and life of the individual himself. A certain patient, of this type, attempts to describe to his physician a peculiar, hitherto undescribed, and even now indescribable sensation "through his right lung." He traces this sensation to what he believes to have been the absorption of a poison some years ago. His line of reasoning is somewhat as follows: 1. The drug was a poison. 2. If he absorbed it he must have been poisoned. 3. If he was poisoned then, he is poisoned now. 4. There is no proof that such a poison cannot produce such a sensation. 5. He has the sensation. Conclusion: He is suffering from poison. In support of this proposition he will spend hours with anyone who will listen. The physician who allows himself to be drawn into the controversy speedily finds himself, instead of giving advice to listening ears, involved in a battle of wits in which he is quite likely to come off second best. He assures the patient, for example, that, as far as scientific methods can establish the fact, the lung is sound.

"But has science established everything? And if it had, is such negative evidence to be weighed against the positive evidence of the sensation in my lung?"

"But the sensation may not be in your lung."

"Can you prove that it is not in my lung?" Folly scores!

On being urged to direct his attention to some other part of his body, he promptly inquires,

"How can I direct my thoughts elsewhere, when the sensation is there to occupy my attention?" Obviously he can not without changing his mental attitude, so folly scores again.

He is assured that if the poison had been absorbed the effects would have passed away long before this time.

"But do the effects of poison always pass away? And can you prove that they have passed away in my case? Is not the sensation positive evidence, since you have allowed that you cannot prove that the sensation does not come from the poison?"

Folly scores again, but the victory is an empty one. The vicious circle continues: Attention magnifies sensation--sensation produces fear--fear increases attention; and throughout runs the insistent thought that his sensations shall conform to his ideal.

If the discussion of such comparatively tangible matters can occupy a large part of one's attention, imagine the result of the insistent desire, on the part of the doubter, to solve such problems as "What is thought?" "What is existence?"

If the windings of this intellectual labyrinth have not too far involved us, we have only to recognize the futility of such arguments, and exercise our will-power in the right direction. If we can bring ourselves to take the initiative, it is as easy to step out of the vicious circle, as for the squirrel to leave his wheel. But unless we grasp the logic of the situation, and take this initiative, no amount of abuse, persuasion, or ridicule will effect our freedom.

* * * * *

A word may be in place regarding the anthropological status of the doubting folly and allied mental states. Men of genius have suffered from them all. A long list may be found in Lombroso's "Man of Genius." Under folie du doute we find, for example, Tolstoi, Manzoni, Flaubert and Amiel.

Lombroso regards genius as degenerative, and places among the signs of degeneration, deviations from the average normal, whether physical or mental. This plan has been quite generally followed. The nomenclature seems to me unfortunate and hardly justified by the facts. I can think of no more potent objection to such inclusive use of the term degenerate, than the fact that Lombroso includes, under the signs of degeneration, the enormous development of the cerebral speech-area in the case of an accomplished orator. If such evolutional spurts are to be deemed degenerative, the fate of the four-leaved clover is sealed.

The application of the term degeneration may be, and should be, it seems to me, limited to the signs, whether physical or mental, which indicate an obviously downward tendency. I have elsewhere suggested, and the suggestion has already found some acceptance, that when the variation is not definitely downward, deviation and deviate be substituted for the unnecessarily opprobrious and often inappropriate terms, degeneration and degenerate.

VII.

HYPOCHONDRIA

Il marche, dort, mange et boit comme tous les autres; mais cela n'empeche pas qu'il soit fort malade.

MOLIERE: Le Malade imaginaire.

The victim of hypochondria may present the picture of health, or may have some real ill regarding which he is unduly anxious. His consultation with a physician is likely to be preceded by letters explaining his exact condition, naming his various consultants and describing the various remedies he has taken. At the time of his visit notes are consulted, lest some detail be omitted. In his description anatomical terms abound; thus, he has pain in his lungs, heart, or kidney, not in his chest or back. Demonstration by the physician of the soundness of these organs is met by argument, at which the hypochondriac is generally adept.

The suggestion that the hypochondriac devotes undue attention to his own condition is met by him with indignant denial. Proposals that he should exercise, travel, engage in games, or otherwise occupy himself, fall on deaf ears, but he is always ready to try a new drug. If a medicine is found with whose ingredients the patient is not already familiar, its use is likely to produce a beneficial effect for a few days, after which the old complaint returns.

The case has come to my attention of a young man who, for fear of taking cold, remains in bed, with the windows of the room tightly closed and a fire constantly burning. He has allowed his hair to grow until it reaches his waist, he is covered with several blankets, wears underclothing under his nightshirt, and refuses to extend his wrist from under the bed-clothes to have his pulse taken.

Such faulty mental habits in minor degree are common. There are those who will not drink from a bottle without first inspecting its mouth for flakes of glass; some will not smoke a cigar which has been touched by another since leaving the factory; some will not shake hands if it can possibly be avoided; another pads his clothing lest he injure himself in falling. Many decline to share the occupations and pleasures of others through fear of possible wet feet, drafts of air, exhaustion, or other calamity. Such tendencies, though falling short of hypochondria, pave the way for it, and, in any event, gradually narrow the sphere of usefulness and pleasure.

No part of the body is exempt from the fears of the hypochondriac, but he is prone to centre his attention upon the obscure and inaccessible organs. The anecdote is told of a physician who had a patient of this type--a robust woman who was never without a long list of ailments. The last time she sent for the doctor, he lost patience with her. As she was telling him how she was suffering from rheumatism, sore throat, nervous indigestion, heart-burn, pains in the back of the head, and what not, he interrupted her:

"Ah," he said in an admiring tone, "what splendid health you must have in order to be able to stand all these complaints!"

The phobias are so closely allied to hypochondria that it will not be out of place to discuss them here. A phobia is an insistent and engrossing fear, without adequate cause as judged by ordinary standards. Familiar instances are fear of open places (agoraphobia), fear of closed places (claustrophobia), and fear of contamination (mysophobia).

The sufferer from agoraphobia cannot bring himself to cross alone an open field or square. The sufferer from claustrophobia will invent any excuse to avoid an elevator or the theatre. When a certain lady was asked if she disliked to go to the theatre or church, she answered, "Not at all, but of course I like to have one foot in the aisle; I suppose everyone does that."

The victim of mysophobia will wash the hands after touching any object, and will, so far as possible, avoid touching objects which he thinks may possibly convey infection. Some use tissue paper to turn the door-knob, some extract coins from the pocket-book with pincers. I have seen a lady in a public conveyance carefully open a piece of paper containing her fare, pour the money into the conductor's hand, carefully fold up the paper so that she should not touch the inside, and afterwards drop it from the tips of her fingers into a rubbish barrel.

The case of a nurse who was dominated by fear of infection has come to my attention. If her handkerchief touched the table it was discarded. She became very adept at moving objects about with her elbows, was finally reduced to helplessness and had to be cared for by others.

Unreasoning fear of one or another mode of conveyance is not rare. It is said that Rossini found it impossible to travel by rail, and that the attempt of a friend to accustom him to it resulted in an attack of faintness (Lombroso).

The sufferer himself realizes, in such cases, that there is no reason in his fear--he knows he can undergo greater dangers with equanimity. Even doubting folly finds no answer to the question why should this danger be shunned and that accepted. The nearest approach to an answer is "I can't," which really means "I haven't."

The origin of the phobia is not always clear, but given the necessary susceptibility, circumstances doubtless dictate the direction the phobia shall take. A startling personal experience, or even reading or hearing of such an experience may start the fear which the insistent thought finally moulds into a fixed habit.

To the hypochondriac who concentrates his attention upon the digestive tract, this part of his body occupies the foreground of all his thoughts. He exaggerates its delicacy of structure and the serious consequences of disturbing it even by an attack of indigestion. A patient to whom a certain fruit was suggested said he could not eat it. Asked what the effect would be, he answered that he did not know, he had not eaten any for twenty years and dared not risk the experiment.

Extreme antipathies to various foods are fostered among this class. A lady told me that she perfectly abominated cereals, that she could not stand vegetables, that she could not bear anything in the shape of an apple, that she could not abide spinach, and that baked beans made her sick at the stomach.

The heart is perhaps the organ most often the object of solicitude on the part of the hypochondriac. When we realize that the pulse may vary in the healthy individual from 60 to over 100, according to circumstances, and that mere excitement may send it to the latter figure, we may appreciate the feelings of one who counts his pulse at frequent intervals and is alarmed if it varies from a given figure.

Inspection of the tongue is a common occupation of the hypochondriac, who is generally more familiar than his medical attendant with the anatomy of this organ.

Insistent desire regarding the temperature is common not only among hypochondriacs, but among others. I do not allude to the internal temperature (though I have been surprised to learn how many people carry a clinical thermometer and use it on themselves from time to time); I refer to the temperature of the room or of the outside air. The wish to feel a certain degree of warmth is so overpowering in some cases that neither work nor play can be carried on unless the thermometer registers the desired figure. A person with this tendency does not venture to mail a letter without donning hat and overcoat; the mere thought of a cold bath causes him to shudder.

Golf has cured many a victim of this obsession. It takes only a few games to teach the most delicately constructed that he can remain for hours in his shirt-sleeves on quite a cold day, and that the cold shower (preferably preceded by a warm one) invigorates instead of depresses him. Further experiment will convince him that he can wear thin underwear and low shoes all winter. Such experiences may encourage him to risk a cold plunge in the morning, followed by a brisk rub and a few simple exercises before dressing.

Morbid fears in themselves produce physical manifestations which add to the discomfort and alarm of the hypochondriac. I allude to the rush of blood to the head, the chill, the mental confusion, and the palpitation. These symptoms are perfectly harmless, and denote only normal circulatory changes. It is true that one cannot at will materially alter his circulation, but he can do so gradually by habit of thought. To convince ourselves of this fact, we need only remember to what a degree blushing becomes modified by change of mental attitude. Similarly, the person who has practiced mental and physical relaxation will find that the blood no longer rushes to his head upon hearing a criticism or remembering a possible source of worry.

The automatic processes of the body are in general performed best when the attention is directed elsewhere. After ordinary care is taken, too minute attention to the digestive apparatus, for example, may retard rather than aid it. Watching the digestion too closely is like pulling up seeds to see if they are growing.

The more attention is paid to the sensations, the more they demand. Nor can the degree of attention they deserve be measured by their own insistence. If one tries the experiment of thinking intently of the end of his thumb, and imagines it is going to sleep, the chances are ten to one that in five minutes it will have all the sensations of going to sleep. If this is true of the healthy-minded individual, how much more must it be so in the person who allows his thoughts to dwell with anxious attention on such parts of his body as may be the immediate seat of his fears. The next step is for various sensations (boring, burning, prickling, stabbing, and the like) to appear spontaneously, and, if attention is paid to them, rapidly to increase in intensity.

It is probable that the mere pressure of part upon part in the body, even the ordinary activity of its organs, would give rise to sensations if we encouraged them. Given an anomalous sensation, or even a pain, for which the physician finds no physical basis, and which, after a term of years, has produced no further appreciable effect than to make one nervous, it is always in place to ask one's self whether the sensation or the pain may not be of this nature.

Medical instructors are continually consulted by students who fear that they have the diseases they are studying. The knowledge that pneumonia produces pain in a certain spot leads to a concentration of attention upon that region which causes any sensation there to give alarm. The mere knowledge of the location of the appendix transforms the most harmless sensations in that region into symptoms of serious menace. The sensible student learns to quiet these fears, but the victim of "hypos" returns again and again for examination, and perhaps finally reaches the point of imparting, instead of obtaining, information, like the patient in a recent anecdote from the _Youth's Companion_:

It seems that a man who was constantly changing physicians at last called in a young doctor who was just beginning his practice.

"I lose my breath when I climb a hill or a steep flight of stairs," said the patient. "If I hurry, I often get a sharp pain in my side. Those are the symptoms of a serious heart trouble."

"Not necessarily, sir," began the physician, but he was interrupted.

"I beg your pardon!" said the patient irritably. "It isn't for a young physician like you to disagree with an old and experienced invalid like me, sir!"

* * * * *

There is no absolute standard for the proper degree of solicitude regarding one's health, but if the habitual invalid possess a physique which would not preclude the average normal individual from being out and about, even at the expense of a pain, a stomach ache, or a cold, there is probably a hypochondriacal element in the case. It is a question of adjustment of effect to cause.

The term "imaginary" is too loosely applied to the sensations of the hypochondriac. This designation is unjustified, and only irritates the sufferer, rouses his antagonism, and undermines his confidence in the judgment of his adviser. He knows that the sensations are there. To call them imaginary is like telling one who inspects an insect through a microscope that the claws do not look enormous; they do look enormous--through the microscope--but this does not make them so. The worrier must learn to realize that he is looking at his sensations, as he does everything else, through a microscope.

If a person living near a waterfall ignores the sound, he soon ceases to notice it, but if he listens for it, it increases, and becomes finally unbearable. Common sense teaches him to concentrate his attention elsewhere; similarly, it demands that the victim of "hypos" disregard his various sensations and devote his attention to outside affairs, unless the sensations are accompanied by obvious physical signs. Instead of running to the doctor, let him do something--ride horseback, play golf, anything requiring exercise out of doors. Let him devote his entire energy to the exercise, and thus substitute the healthy sensations of fatigue and hunger for the exaggerated pains and the anomalous sensations which are fostered by self-study. Let him remember moreover, that nature will stand an enormous amount of outside abuse, but resents being kept under close surveillance.

In practicing the neglect of the sensations, one should not allow his mind to dwell on the possibility that he is overlooking something serious, but rather on the danger of his becoming "hipped," a prey to his own doubts and fears, and unable to accomplish anything in life beyond catering to his own morbid fancies.

* * * * *

Turning now to the bibliographic study of hypochondria, an interesting and characteristic contrast is offered between Huxley, who called himself a hypochondriac, but apparently was not, and Carlyle, who resented the imputation, though it apparently had some justification in fact.

With regard to Huxley,--the only basis for the diagnosis hypochondria in a given case, is undoubted evidence, by letter or conversation, that the question of health is given undue prominence. I have looked carefully through the volume of Huxley's letters (published by his son), without definitely establishing this diagnosis. The state of his health and the question of his personal comfort received comparatively little attention. Whatever suffering Huxley endured he seems to have accepted in a philosophical and happy spirit, thus:

"It is a bore to be converted into a troublesome invalid even for a few weeks, but I comfort myself with my usual reflection on the chances of life, 'Lucky it is no worse.' Any impatience would have been checked by what I heard about ... this morning ... that he has sunk into hopeless idiocy. A man in the prime of life!"

With regard to Carlyle,--it is true, as claimed by Gould (_Biographic Clinics_, 1903) that he showed every evidence of eyestrain with resulting symptoms, particularly headache. This does not, however, preclude his having had hypochondria also, and in view of the violent and reiterated complaints running through his letters it seems quite credible that Froude's estimate of his condition was not far wrong. Surely, unless Carlyle was merely trying his pen without intending to be taken seriously, he devoted to the question of health a degree of attention which may be fairly adjudged undue.

The first letter I quote (from those cited by Gould in fortifying his position) is of special interest as presenting in rather lurid terms Carlyle's ideal of health. After reading this letter one cannot help suspecting that the discomforts so vividly described in his other letters were compared by him with this ideal rather than with those of the average individual.

"In the midst of your zeal and ardor,... remember the care of health.... It would have been a very great thing for me if I had been able to consider that health is a thing to be attended to continually, that you are to regard that as the very highest of all temporal things for you. There is no kind of achievement you could make in the world that is equal to perfect health. What to it are nuggets and millions'? The French financier said 'Why is there no sleep to be sold!' Sleep was not in the market at any quotation.... I find that you could not get any better definition of what 'holy' really is than 'healthy.' Completely healthy; mens sana in corpore sano. A man all lucid, and in equilibrium. His intellect a clear mirror geometrically plane, brilliantly sensitive to all objects and impressions made on it and imaging all things in their correct proportions; not twisted up into convex or concave, and distorting everything so that he cannot see the truth of the matter, without endless groping and manipulation: healthy, clear, and free and discerning truly all around him."

The following extracts illustrate his attitude toward his physical shortcomings, whatever they may have been.

... "A prey to nameless struggles and miseries, which have yet a kind of horror in them to my thoughts, three weeks without any kind of sleep, from impossibility to be free from noise."

"I sleep irregularly here, and feel a little, very little, more than my usual share of torture every day. What the cause is would puzzle me to explain. I take exercise sufficient daily; I attend with rigorous minuteness to the quality of my food; I take all the precautions that I can, yet still the disease abates not."

"Ill-health, the most terrific of all miseries."

"Grown sicker and sicker.... I want health, health, health! On this subject I am becoming quite furious.... If I do not soon recover, I am miserable forever and ever. They talk of the benefit of health from a moral point of view. I declare solemnly, without exaggeration, that I impute nine-tenths of my present wretchedness, and rather more than nine-tenths of all my faults, to this infernal disorder in the stomach."

"Bilious, too, in these smothering windless days."

"Broke down in the park; konnte _nichts mehr_, being sick and weak beyond measure."

"Many days of suffering, of darkness, of despondency.... Ill-health has much to do with it."

"Occasionally sharp pain (something cutting hard, grasping me around the heart).... Something from time to time were, all around the region of the heart, and strange dreams haunting me."

"There is a shivering precipitancy in me, which makes emotion of any kind a thing to be shunned. It is my nerves, my nerves.... Such a nervous system as I have.... Thomas feeling in his breast for comfort and finding bilious fever.... All palpitating, fluttered with sleeplessness and drug-taking, etc.... Weary and worn with dull blockheadism, chagrin (next to no sleep the night before)."

"A head _full of air_; you know that wretched physical feeling; I had been concerned with drugs, had awakened at five, etc. It is absolute martyrdom."

"A huge nightmare of indigestion, insomnia, and fits of black impatience with myself and others,--self chiefly.... I am heartily sick of my dyspeptic bewilderment and imprisonment."

"Alas! Alas! I ought to be wrapped in cotton wool, and laid in a locked drawer at present. I can stand nothing. I am really ashamed of the figure I cut."

Froude's statements regarding Carlyle's condition are as follows:

"... The simple natural life, the 'wholesome air, the daily rides or drives, the poor food,... had restored completely the functions of a stomach never so far wrong as he had imagined.... Afterwards he was always impatient, moody, irritable, violent. These humours were in his nature, and he could no more be separated from them than his body could leap off its shadow.... He looked back to it as the happiest and wholesomest home that he had ever known. He could do fully twice as much work there, he said, as he could ever do afterwards in London."

"... If his liver occasionally troubled him, livers trouble most of us as we advance in life, and his actual constitution was a great deal stronger than that of ordinary men.... Why could not Carlyle, with fame and honor and troops of friends, and the gates of a great career flung open before him, and a great intellect and a conscience untroubled by a single act which he need regret, bear and forget too? Why indeed! The only answer is that Carlyle was Carlyle."

These observations carry weight as representing the impartial and judicial estimate of a careful observer desiring only accurately to picture Carlyle as he was. The only logical conclusion, it seems to me, was that Carlyle, in addition to ocular defect with its legitimate consequences, was weighed down by worry over the failure to realize his own exaggerated ideal of health, that he devoted an undue degree of attention to this subject and was unduly anxious about it--in other words, that he had decided hypochondriacal tendencies.

VIII.

NEURASTHENIA

It was a common saying of Myson that men ought not to investigate things from words, but words from things; for that things are not made for the sake of words, but words for things.

Diogenes Laertius.

This term (properly, though not commonly, accented upon the penult), was introduced by Beard to designate the large class of over-worked and worried who crowded his consulting room. The word is derived from the Greek neuron nerve, and astheneia weakness.

Among the symptoms of this disorder have been included disorders of digestion and circulation, muscular weakness, pains, flushes and chills, and anomalous sensations of every variety. It has been especially applied to cases showing such mental peculiarities as morbid self-study, fear of insanity and the various other phobias, scruples, and doubts with which we have become familiar.

The "American Disease" has been adopted abroad, and volumes have been devoted to it. Neurasthenia has been divided into cerebral, spinal, and otherwise, according as the fears and sensations of the patient are referred to one or another part of his body. While the term neurasthenia is becoming daily more familiar to the general public, it is being, on the whole, used, except as a convenient handle, rather less among neurologists. [Footnote: In substantiation of this statement I need only cite the recent contribution of my friend, Dr. Dana, on the "Partial Passing of Neurasthenia."] The question has arisen whether the symptoms of neurasthenia are always due to simple exhaustion. Advice regarding method, as well as amount, of work, is coming into vogue. Peterson, in a letter published in _Collier's Weekly_ (November 9, 1907) thus arraigns a patient who has told him he is a practical business man, and that his mind has been so occupied with serious matters that he has been unable to attend to his health.

"You, practical! you, a business man! Why, you never had a serious thought in your life until now--at least not since you were a lad in the country.... Since boyhood you have never given a serious thought to health, home, wife, children, education, art, science, racial progress, or to the high destiny of man. You are simply a collector of money for its own sake, with no appreciation of what it might represent if you were really serious and really a business man or man of affairs. There are many like you in our asylum wards, where they are known as chronic maniacs. Here is one who collects bits of glass, old corks, and pieces of string. There sits another with a lap full of pebbles, twigs and straws."

Courtney (in Pyle's "Personal Hygiene") says, "The brain is an organ which, under proper training, is capable of performing an immense amount of work, provided only that the work is of a varied character and does not produce a corresponding amount of mental disquietude. The importance of the emotions, especially the depressing emotions such as grief, anxiety, and worry, as factors in the brain exhaustion, cannot easily be overestimated."

The obvious corollary to this proposition is that the constitutional worrier is likely to break down under an amount of work which produces no such effect upon the average normal individual.

The only quarrel I have with the name neurasthenia is that it diverts attention from the real condition oftenest to be treated, namely, the faulty mental tendency, and directs attention to an assumed debility which may or may not exist. Misdirected energy, rather than weakness, is the difficulty with one who is ready and anxious to walk miles to satisfy a doubt, or to avoid crossing an open square, and who will climb a dozen flights of stairs rather than be shut up in an elevator. Even the exhaustion that follows long attention to business is quite as often due to worry and allied faulty mental habits as to the work itself. In most cases the phobias, the doubts, and the scruples, instead of being the result of breakdown, must be counted among its principal causes.

This is why simple rest and abstinence from work so often fail to accomplish the cure that should follow if the exhaustion were due simply to overwork. In the "neurasthenic" rest from work only redoubles the worries, the doubts and the scruples, and the obsession to improve his time only adds to his nervous exhaustion. If a European trip is undertaken, the temperament responsible for the original breakdown causes him to rush from gallery to gallery, from cathedral to cathedral, so that no moment may be lost. Not infrequently it so happens that the patient returns more jaded than ever.

The neurasthenic is not infrequently a confirmed obsessive, with all the faulty mental habits of this temperament. If he cannot make up his mind it is not because he is tired, but because this is his natural mental trend. If he drums, twitches, and walks the floor, these movements are not always due to exhaustion, but are habits peculiar to the temperament, habits well worth an effort to eliminate while in health, since they doubtless, through precluding bodily repose, contribute their mite toward the very exhaustion of which they are supposed to be the result. If he cannot sleep it is not simply because he is tired, but because he is so constituted that he cannot bring himself to let go his hold on consciousness until he has straightened out his tangles. If, in addition, one has the hypochondriacal tendency, he may worry himself into complete wakefulness by the thought that he has already irreparably injured himself by missing something of the mystic number, eight or nine, or whatever he may deem the number of hours' sleep essential to health.

It is important that the overwrought business or professional man realize the importance of undertaking no more than he can accomplish without fret and worry; the importance of taking proper vacations before he is tired out; the importance of learning to divert his mind, while he can still do so, into channels other than those connected with his business; above all, the importance of cultivating the faculty of relaxing, and of dismissing doubts, indecisions and fears. He must cultivate what my colleague Dr. Paul succinctly terms "the art of living with yourself as you are." If he would "last out" he must learn to proceed with single mind upon whatever work he undertakes, and with equal singleness of mind apply himself, out of hours, to other occupation or diversion, preferably in the open air. For the most effective work, as well as for peace of mind, it is essential that every thought of one's office be shut out by other interests when there is no actual business requiring attention. Mental relaxation is materially hampered by such persistent thoughts of one's place of business as those cited by Dr. Knapp:

"A striking instance of the sort was related to me by a friend remarkably free from any psychopathic taint. It often happens that he does scientific work in the evening at the Agassiz Museum. When he leaves for the night he puts out the gas and then stands and counts slowly up to a given number until his eyes are used to the darkness, in order that he may detect any spark of fire that may have started while he was at work. This is his invariable custom, but it sometimes happens that when he goes back home so strong a feeling of doubt comes over him lest he may that once have omitted to do this, that he is uncomfortable until he returns to the museum to make sure."

Among the predisposing causes for nervous breakdown none is more potent than the inability of the obsessive to adapt himself to change of plan, and to reconcile himself to criticism, opposition, and the various annoyances incident to his occupation.

In dealing with others the following suggestion of Marcus Aurelius may come in play:

"When a man has done thee any wrong, immediately consider with what opinion about good or evil he has done wrong. For when thou hast seen this, thou wilt pity him, and neither wonder nor be angry." Again, in this connection the lines of Cowper are pertinent:

"The modest, sensible and well-bred man Will not affront me, and no other can."

Pope, also, who is said not always to have followed his own good counsel, contributes a verse which may serve a turn:

"At ev'ry trifle scorn to take offense, That always shows great pride, or little sense."

The practice of such commonplace philosophy (which, to be effective, should be ready for immediate use, not stored away for later reflection), together with training against faulty mental states studied in these pages, will go far toward relieving the mental perturbation that unfits for effective work, and contributes to "neurasthenia."

During an hour's delay, caused by the failure of another to keep an appointment, I formulated the following maxim:

"These are the annoyances incident to my business; to fret when they occur means that I cannot manage my business without friction."

This may not appeal to the reader, but for me it has proved as good an hour's work as I ever did. Since that time, on the occurrence of similar sources of provocation, I have found it necessary to go no farther than "These are the annoyances," to restore the needful balance. When we allow our gorge to rise at ordinary sources of discomfort, it implies that we are prepared only for our affairs to run with perfect smoothness. This represents the insistent idea carried to an absurdity.

At the risk of losing caste with the critical I cannot forbear sharing with the reader an inelegant maxim which has more than once prevented an access of rage upon the blunder of a subordinate: "If he had our brains he'd have our job."

Spinoza says: "The powerlessness of man to govern and restrain his emotions I call servitude. For a man who is controlled by his emotions is not his own master but is mastered by fortune, under whose power he is often compelled, though he sees the better, to follow the worse." The same philosopher in counselling self-restraint adds:

"The mind's power over the emotions consists, first, in the actual knowledge of the emotions." Again: "An emotion which is a passion ceases to be a passion as soon as we form a clear and distinct idea of it." The meaning of this dictum I first realized on experiencing the magical effect of the line of thought suggested by the delayed appointment.

* * * * *

Communion with Nature has a peculiarly soothing effect on tired and jangled nerves. My friend, Dr. Harold Williams, tells me that among his main reliances for tired and overwrought women are the _reading of children's books_, and working in the garden. Peterson thus advises his busy patient:

"A small farm in a simple community would be for you an asset of immeasurable value from the standpoint of health and spiritual rejuvenation. But true simplicity should be the rigorous order of that country life. A chateau by the sea, with a corps of gardeners, a retinue of servants, and yachts and automobiles, would prove a disastrous expedient.

"In that quiet retreat you should personally and tenderly learn to know each rosebud, shrub, vine, creeper, tree, rock, glade, dell, of your own estate. You should yourself design the planting, paths, roads, the flower-garden, the water-garden, the wood-garden, the fernery, the lily-pond, the wild-garden, and the kitchen garden."

Not everyone is so happily situated as to be able to follow this advice in its entirety, but many can make a modest effort in this direction: the kitchen-garden may appeal to some who have no appreciation for the wild flowers, and who scorn to cultivate such tastes.

One warning is, however, here in order: The cultivation of the garden or the field for utilitarian purposes is inevitably associated with the maxim, "Hoe out your row"--an excellent maxim for the idle and disorderly, but not to be taken too literally by the over-exacting and methodical business man who is trying to make the radical change in his view of life necessary to free his mind from the incubus of worry. Nor must the amateur husbandman scan with too anxious eye the weather map and the clouds. If he mind these warnings he may learn to say,--

"For me kind Nature wakes her genial pow'r, Suckles each herb, and spreads out ev'ry flower, Annual for me, the grape, the rose renew, The juice nectareous, and the balmy dew."

The over-conscientious individual may object that it is selfish to consider his own comfort when he has work to do for others. But expending too freely of our nervous energies, even in a good cause, is like giving to charity so much of our substance that we in turn are obliged to lean on others for support.

In properly conserving our own energy we may be lightening the ultimate burden of others. There is no place for selfishness in Haeckel's philosophy regarding the proper balance between duty to one's self and duty to others. Nor was selfishness a failing of the Quaker poet who idealized

"The flawless symmetry of man, The poise of heart and mind."

IX.

SLEEPLESSNESS

He shall enjoy the same tranquility in his sleep as when awake.

Digby's Epicurus, Maxim xl.

Sleeplessness is due, in the majority of cases, to a faulty habit of mind. The preparation for a sleepless night begins with the waking hours, is continued through the day, and reaches its maximum when we cease from the occupations which have in some degree diverted our attention from harassing thoughts, and retire, to struggle, in darkness and solitude, with the worries, doubts, regrets, and forebodings, which now assume gigantic and fantastic shapes.

He who would sleep at night must regulate his day, first, by not undertaking more than he can accomplish without undue stress, and, second, by carrying through what he does undertake, as far as he may, without the running accompaniment of undue solicitude, anxious doubts, and morbid fears discussed in the preceding sections. It is futile to expect that a fretful, impatient, and over-anxious frame of mind, continuing through the day and every day, will be suddenly replaced at night by the placid and comfortable mental state which shall insure a restful sleep.

Before proceeding, then, to the immediate measures for inducing sleep, let us consider the suitable preparatory measures.

The nervous breakdown which precludes sleep is oftener due to worry than to work. Nor should the sufferer jump too quickly to the conclusion that it is the loss of sleep rather than the worry that makes him wretched. It is astonishing how much sleep can be lost without harm, provided its loss is forgotten, and how much work can be carried on without extreme fatigue, provided it be undertaken with confidence and pursued without impatience. It is, however, essential that the work be varied and, at due intervals, broken. Trainers for athletic contests know that increasing practice without diversion defeats its end, and particularly insist upon cessation of violent effort directly before the final test. Why should we not treat our minds as well as our bodies?

The active and over-scrupulous business or professional man who allows no time for rest or recreation, who can confer no responsibility upon his subordinates, who cultivates no fad, and is impatient of every moment spent away from his occupation, is in danger of eventually "going stale," and having to spend a longer and less profitable vacation in a sanitarium than would have sufficed to avert the disaster. Nor will he find it easy to change his sleep-habit with the change of residence. It behooves him to change that habit while still at work, as a step toward averting breakdown.

It will harm few of us to take a bird's eye view of our affairs at stated intervals, and ask ourselves if the time has not arrived when it will be a saving of time and money as well as worry for us to delegate more of the details, and more even of the responsibilities, to others, concentrating our own energies upon such tasks as we are now peculiarly qualified to undertake. To the man determined to accomplish a lifetime of work before he rests, there is food for thought in the following anecdote:

When Pyrrhus was about to sail for Italy, Cineas, a wise and good man, asked him what were his intentions and expectations.

"To conquer Rome," said Pyrrhus.

"And what will you do next, my lord?"

"Next I will conquer Italy."

"And after that?"

"We will subdue Carthage, Macedonia, all Africa, and all Greece."

"And when we have conquered all we can, what shall we do?"

"Do? Why, then we will sit down and spend our time in peace and comfort."

"Ah, my lord," said the wise Cineas, "what prevents our being in peace and comfort now?"

The time to take a vacation is before one is exhausted. If one is discontented during his vacation, he should take it, none the less, as a matter of duty, not expecting to enjoy every moment of it, but contenting himself with the anticipation of greater pleasure in the resumption of his duties. He should cultivate an interest in out-door occupation or some study that carries him into the fields or woods. Aside from the time on shipboard, the worst possible vacation for the over-worked business or professional man is the trip to Europe, if spent in crowding into the shortest possible time the greatest possible amount of information on matters artistic, architectural, and historic.

No one can acquire the habit of sleep who has not learned the habit of concentration, of devoting himself single-minded to the matter in hand. If we practice devoting our minds, as we do our bodies, to one object at a time, we shall not only accomplish more, but with less exhaustion. Training in this direction will help us, on retiring, to view sleep as our present duty, and a sufficient duty, without taking the opportunity at that time to adjust (or to try to adjust) all our tangles, to review our past sources of discomfort, and to speculate upon the ills of the future.

A walk, a bath, a few gymnastic exercises, will often serve a useful purpose before retiring, but if they are undertaken in a fretful and impatient spirit, and are accompanied by doubts of their effectiveness, and the insistent thought that sleep will not follow these or any other procedure, they are likely to accomplish little.

The best immediate preparation for sleep is the confidence that one will sleep, and indifference if one does not. It is an aid in the adoption of this frame of mind to learn that many have for years slept only a few hours per night, without noticeable impairment of their health or comfort. Neither unbroken nor long-continued sleep, however desirable, is essential to longevity or efficiency. This is illustrated by the following examples:

Joseph A. Willard, for nearly half a century Clerk of the Court in Suffolk County, and a well-known figure on the streets of Boston, died in his eighty-eighth year. He was active and alert in the performance of his daily duties up to their discontinuance shortly before his death. He kept, meantime, records of the temperature, weather, and condition of the streets, at all hours of the night, and every night, for many years before the establishment of the weather bureau. So reliable were these records regarded by the courts that they were often appealed to in the trial of cases, and their accuracy never questioned by either party in the suit. I publish these facts by the permission of his son.

George T. Angell, the well-known humanitarian, than whom few, if any, have led a more busy life, when in his sixty-ninth year wrote as follows:

"For the benefit of those who do not [take narcotics, opiates, anesthetics] I will say that I suppose there are very few in this country who have slept less than I have; but I have never taken anything to stupefy, while thousands of good sleepers I have known have long since gone to the last sleep that knows no waking here. It was undoubtedly wise to change my professional life from court to office practice: but in other matters I was compelled to choose between living the life of a vegetable, or losing sleep; and I chose the latter."

Mr. Angell is now eighty-four, still actively engaged in affairs, and allows me to add that during the past six years he has gone for a week at a time with no sleep; for three months at a time he has not averaged more than two hours in twenty-four; he does not remember having ever had a good night's sleep. Mrs. Angell states that, with one exception, she has never known him to sleep through the night.

It is worth while to remember these experiences before resorting to drugs for sleeplessness.

I have somewhere seen it stated that a prominent divine attributed his happy and green old age to the fact that he slept a certain number of hours every night. Against this statement must be set the reflection that many another old gentleman can fairly attribute his comfort, in part at least, to an attitude of indifference toward the unessentials, among which I suspect must be included the question whether we average eight hours of sleep or materially less.

Let us now consider some of the faulty mental habits directly affecting sleep itself. First comes the compulsive thought that one must sleep _now_, and the impatient count of the wakeful hours supposed to be irrecoverably lost from the coveted number. This insistence in itself precludes sleep. The thought, "No matter if I don't sleep to-night; I will some other night," will work wonders in the direction of producing sleep to-night.

The continuance of any given position, completely relaxed, in bed, even without unconsciousness, is more restful than tossing about. The mere experiment of remaining immobile in a certain position as long as possible, and concentrating the mind on the thought, "I am getting sleepy, I am going to sleep," will oftener produce the desired result than watching the proverbial sheep follow one another over the wall. Training during the day in restraining nervous movements is an aid in acquiring the ability to do this.

This is a field in which self-suggestion is of definite value. Everyone appreciates the effect on sleep of the "state of mind" when he has passed a succession of sleepless hours followed by a sudden tendency to somnolence at the time for rising. The problem is to acquire the frame of mind without waiting for circumstances. To demonstrate the effect of faulty suggestion combined with restlessness on awaking in the night, try the following:

EXPERIMENT I.--Place yourself on the face and from this point turn rapidly in a complete circle backwards from right to left until you are again on the face. Pause several times and say to yourself rapidly "I cannot sleep in this position." The result of the experiment is practically uniform. The rapid movement and the suggestion prevent sleep.

To demonstrate the effect of bodily relaxation combined with correct suggestion, in promoting sleep try--

EXPERIMENT II.--Start in the same position as Experiment I. Traverse the same circle, prolonging each pause with body relaxed, and substituting at each pause the suggestion, "I can sleep in any position," repeated a number of times deliberately and as if you meant it. The restful pose and the suggestion generally induce sleep long before the circle is completed.

Next comes the compulsive thought that we cannot sleep until everything is "squared up" and all mental pictures completed. The story is told that a gentleman took a room in the hotel next another who was notoriously fussy. He remembered this fact after dropping one boot carelessly to the floor, and laid the other gently down. After a pause he heard a rap on the door and a querulous, "For heaven's sake, drop the other boot, or I can't get to sleep."

Many find themselves unable to sleep until the whole household is accounted for and the house locked up for the night, until certain news is received, and the like. The same tendency postpones sleep until all affairs are straightened out in the mind, as well as in reality. A little reflection shows how indefinite must be the postponement of sleep under such conditions.

No training is more important for the victim of compulsive tendencies than the practice of trusting something to chance and the morrow, and reconciling himself to the fact that at no time, in this world, will all things be finally adjusted to his satisfaction.

The habit of dismissing, at will, disagreeable thoughts is a difficult but not impossible acquisition. Arthur Benson in "The Thread of Gold" relates the following anecdotes:

"When Gladstone was asked, 'But don't you find you lie awake at night, thinking how you ought to act, and how you ought to have acted?' he answered, 'No, I don't; where would be the use of that?'"

"Canon Beadon [who lived to be over one hundred] said to a friend that the secret of long life in his own case was that he had never thought of anything unpleasant after ten o'clock at night."

The insistent desire to sleep in a certain bed, with a certain degree of light or darkness, heat or cold, air or absence of air, is detrimental. This is in line with the desire to eat certain foods only, at a certain table, and at a certain time. The man who loses his appetite if dinner is half an hour late is unable again to sleep if once waked up. This individual must say to himself, "Anyone can stand what he likes; it takes a philosopher to stand what he does not like," and try at being a philosopher instead of a sensitive plant.

Ina

certain noises are continued must be similarly combated. If one goes from place to place in search of the quiet spot for sleep, he may finally find quiet itself oppressive, or worse yet, may be kept awake by hearing his own circulation, from which escape is out of the question. He who finds himself persistently out of joint with his surroundings will do well to ponder the language of the Chinese philosopher:

"The legs of the stork are long, the legs of the duck are short: you cannot make the legs of the stork short, neither can you make the legs of the duck long. Why worry?"

With regard to the character of sleep itself, the attitude of our mind in sleep is dominated, to a degree, at least, by its attitude in the waking hours. It is probable that during profound sleep the mind is inactive, and that dreams occur only during the transition-state from profound sleep to wakefulness. It is conceivable that in the ideal sleep there is only one such period, but ordinarily there occur many such periods during the night; for the uneasy sleeper the night may furnish a succession of such periods, with comparatively little undisturbed rest, hence his dreams seem to him continuous. The character of the pictures and suggestions of dreams, though in new combinations, are largely dependent on our daily experiences. Is it not, then, worth while to encourage, during our waking hours, as far as is consistent with our duties, such thoughts as are restful and useful, rather than those which serve no purpose but annoyance.

If we will, we can select our thoughts as we do our companions.

X.

OCCUPATION NEUROSIS

Be not ashamed, to be helped; for it is thy business to do thy duty like a soldier in the assault on a town. How, then, if being lame thou canst not mount up on the battlement alone, but with the help of another it is possible?

Marcus Aurelius.

The insistent and over-conscientious habit of mind plays so large a part in the so-called occupation neuroses that a brief discussion of their nature may here be in place.

The best-known form of this distressing malady is "writer's cramp." Upon this subject the proverbially dangerous little knowledge has been already acquired; a fuller knowledge may give comfort rather than alarm, and may even lead to the avoidance of this and allied nervous disorders.

The term "writer's cramp" has unduly emphasized a feature, namely, the cramp, which is neither the most common nor the most troublesome among the symptoms resulting from over-use of a part. In occupation neuroses, other than those produced by the use of the pen, pain, weakness, and numbness are at least equally prominent, and even in writer's cramp the "neuralgic" form is common.

The fact is generally realized that this type of disorder is particularly frequent among persons of nervous temperament. The reason is twofold, first, the resistance of such individuals is less than the average, second, the insistent habit of mind leads them to overdo. It is against the latter factor that our efforts may to advantage be directed.

I have in mind the case of a lady who complained of severe pain in the right arm with no apparent physical cause. The pain, at first appearing only when the arm was placed in a certain position, finally became almost constant. She denied excessive use of the arm, but her husband stated that she plied the needle to such an extent that it caused the family distress. This she indignantly denied, and fortified her position by the statement that she only took short stitches! Further inquiry elicited the acknowledgment that she did so because she could no longer take long ones. This is a fair example of an occupation neurosis.

Some time ago, after long continued and over-conscientious effort to satisfy the requirements of an athletic instructor, I acquired what is known as a "golf arm." Efforts at its relief were unavailing. A vigorous course of massage only increased the pain. I finally asked a friend what they did in England when a golf player suffered this annoyance. He replied that no golf player ever did so; when it occurred among others the arm was placed in wool for three months, at the end of which time a single movement of swinging the club was made; if this movement caused pain the treatment was renewed for another three months. I did not suppose he intended the advice to be taken literally, but followed it, except as regarded the wool, and I verily believe that I should otherwise have been experimenting with the treatment of golf arm to-day.

My friend's advice indicates the general experience with occupation neuroses including writer's cramp, for which every imaginable measure has been tried, only to be replaced by protracted abstinence from the use of the pen. The attempt to use the left hand proves, as a rule, only temporarily efficacious. The speedy appearance of symptoms in the left hand emphasizes the fact that it is tired brain, as well as the tired muscle, that rebels.

The ranks of every profession, and of every trade, are daily depleted of the most promising among their members, whose zeal has outrun their discretion;

their over-worked brains and hands have succumbed under the incessant strain of tasks, often self-imposed.

It is hard, but essential, for the sufferer from an occupation neurosis to abandon frantic efforts at combining treatment with continuance of labor. He must bring all his philosophy to bear on the temporary, but complete, abandonment of his chosen occupation, at whatever loss to himself or others.

To avoid this contingency the over-conscientious worker will do well to modify his ambition, and lower his pride if needful, consoling himself with the reflection that an occasional interruption of his labor, even at material loss, may be replaced by years of future usefulness. Cowper says:

"'Tis thus the understanding takes repose In indolent vacuity of thought, And rests, and is refreshed."

XI.

THE WORRIER AT HOME

Small habits, well pursued betimes, May reach the dignity of crimes.

Hannah More.

More than one "sunbeam" and "life of the party" in society is the "cross patch" and "fuss budget" of the home. His gracious smiles and quips abroad are matched at home by darkened brows and moody silence, only broken by conversation of the italicized variety: "Will it ever stop raining?" "_Can't_ you see that I am busy?" "What are you doing?" and the like. Whatever banner is exhibited to the outside world, the motto at home seems to be "Whatever is, is wrong." Defects, carefully overlooked when dining out, are called with peculiar unction to the attention of the housekeeper of the home, whose worry to please is only matched by the "sunbeam's" fear that she shall think him satisfied with what is placed before him.

"There's something kind of pitiful about a man that growls Because the sun beats down too hot, because the wild wind howls, Who never eats a meal but that the cream ain't thick enough, The coffee ain't been settled right, or else the meat's too tough--

Poor chap! He's just the victim of Fate's oldest, meanest trick, You'll see by watching mules and men, they don't need brains to kick."

Chicago Interocean.

Add to the "kicking habit" the insistence that each member of the family must be reminded at frequent intervals of his peculiar weaknesses, and that the discussion of uncomfortable topics, long since worn threadbare, must be reopened at every available opportunity, and the adage is justified, "be it ever so humble, there's no place like home."

Try the following suggestion on approaching the house after a hard day's work. Say to yourself, "Why tired and cross? Why not tired and good-natured?" The result may startle the family and cause inquiries for your health, but "Don't Worry," if it does; console yourself with the thought they will like you none the less for giving them a glimpse of that sunny nature of which they have often heard.

As a further preparation for the evening meal, and the evening, by way of alleviating the mental and physical discomfort following a trying day, one is surprised by the effectiveness of taking a bath and changing all the clothing. This treatment, in fact, almost offers a sure cure, but the person who would be most benefited thereby, is the person so obsessed to pursue the miserable tenor of his way that he scouts the suggestion that he thus bestir himself, instead of sinking into the easy chair. He may, however, accept the suggestion that simply changing the shoes and stockings is extremely restful, when reminded that if he had worn kid gloves all day he would be relieved to free his hands from the incubus, and, if gloves must still be worn, to put on a cool pair.

It is a further aid to physical, and indirectly to mental, comfort, if one can learn to wear low shoes and the thinnest of underwear the year round; the former offer a panacea for fidgets; the latter lessens the perspiration, which increases the susceptibility to drafts, and to even moderate lowering of temperature. The prevailing belief that this procedure is dangerous is disproved by the experience of the many who have given it a thorough trial.

The insistent belief of the neurotic that he cannot acquire this habit is touched upon in the chapter on Worry and Obsession. If he thinks he is "taking cold," let him throw back his shoulders and take a few deep breaths, or if convenient, a few exercises, instead of doubling the weight of his underwear, and in the long run he will find that he has not only increased his comfort, but has lessened, rather than increased, the number of his colds.

Much of the worry of the home is retrospective. "If I had only made Mary wear her rubbers,"--"If we had only invested in Calumet & Hecla at 25,"--"If we had only sent John to college," represent a fruitful source of family discomfort. The morbid rhyme is familiar to all:

"Of all sad words of tongue or pen, The saddest these, 'It might have been.'"

I should be glad to learn of any advantage accruing from the indulgence of this attitude toward the bygone. A happier and more sensible habit of mind may be attained by equal familiarity with the following:

"Add this suggestion to the verse, 'It might have been a great deal worse.'"

A fruitful source of discomfort for the worrier at home is the absence of occupation. He looks forward to mental rest after using his brain all day, but there is no rest for him unless in sleep. The most valuable rest he could give his mind would be to occupy it with something worth while, yet not so strenuous as to cause solicitude. As Saleeby points out, the mock worry of a game is a good antidote for the real worry of life, and a game is far better than nothing, unless the player make, in turn, a work of his play, in which case worry continues.

The hardest task for the worrier at home is to get away from home. With advancing years the temptation grows upon us to spend our evenings by the fireside, to make no new friends and seek no new enjoyments. But this unbroken habit is neither the best preparation for a happy old age, nor the best method of counteracting present worry. Nor should one stop to decide whether the special entertainment in question will be worthwhile--he must depend rather on the realization that if he accepts most opportunities he will be, on the whole, the gainer.

The man whose occupation keeps him in-doors all day should make special effort to pass some time in the open air, if possible walking or driving to and from his place of business, and taking at least a stroll in the evening.

As more than one writer has suggested, the best resource is the fad. The fad will prove an inestimable boon after withdrawing from active work, but it should be commenced long before one discontinues business, else the chances are that he will never take it up, but will fret away his time like the average man who retires from an occupation which has engrossed his attention.

The fad should not be pursued too strenuously, or its charm is lost. A lady once told me that she had given up studying flowers because she found she could not master botany in the time at her disposal. Another sees no use in taking up history unless he can become an authority on some epoch. Another declines to study because he can never overtake the college graduate. But one of the best informed men of my acquaintance had no college education. One of his fads was history, with which he was far more familiar than any but the exceptional college man, outside the teachers of that branch of learning.

The usefulness of the fad does not depend upon the perfection attained in its pursuit, but upon the pleasure in its pursuit, and upon the diversion of the mind from its accustomed channels. The more completely one learns to concentrate his thoughts on an avocation_, the more enthusiasm and effectiveness he can bring to bear on his vocation in its turn. A fad that occupies the hands, such as carpentering, turning, or photography, is peculiarly useful if one's taste runs in that direction.

One handicap in cultivating the fad is the lack of interest on the part of our associates, but if we become genuinely interested in any fad that is at all worth while, we shall inevitably add new acquaintances likely to prove at least as interesting as those of our present friends, who have no thoughts outside their daily round of toil. The more fads one cultivates, so long as he avoids the obsession to obtrude them at all times and places, the more interesting he will, in his turn, become to others.

The over-solicitude that defeats its own end, in the case of a parent, has been admirably portrayed by Arthur Benson in "Beside Still Waters,"-- "there was nothing in the world that he more desired than the company and the sympathy of his children; but he had, beside this, an intense and tremulous sense of his responsibility toward them. He attached an undue importance to small indications of character, and thus the children were seldom at ease with their father, because he rebuked them constantly, and found frequent fault, doing almost violence to his tenderness, not from any pleasure in censoriousness, but from a terror, that was almost morbid, of the consequences of the unchecked development of minute tendencies."

Something must be left to natural growth, and to fortune, even in such important matters as the rearing of children.

XII.

THE WORRIER ON HIS TRAVELS

After all, is it not a part of the fine art of living to take the enjoyment of the moment as it comes without lamenting that it is not something else?

LILIAN WHITING: Land of Enchantment.

In no phase of life is the worrying and the "fussy" habit more noticeable than in travel. This is, perhaps, partly because the lack of self-confidence, which so often unsettles the worrier, is peculiarly effective when he has relinquished the security of his accustomed anchorage. This applies surely to the over-solicitous attention paid by the traveler to the possible dangers of rail and sea. Here is a verse from Wallace Irwin:

"'Suppose that this here vessel,' says the skipper with a groan, 'Should lose 'er bearin's, run away and bump upon a stone; Suppose she'd shiver and go down when save ourselves we could'nt.' The mate replies, 'Oh, blow me eyes! Suppose agin she shouldn't?'"

A common direction taken by the worrying habit, in the traveler, is that of taking in advance each step of the journey, preparing for every contingency, and suffering beforehand every imaginable hardship and inconvenience. I do not vouch for the story (though I can match it without going far afield) of the gentleman who abandoned his trip from Paris to Budapesth because he found he would be delayed in Vienna six hours, "too long time to wait in the station, and not long enough to go to the hotel." It is the imperative duty of every traveler to discover interests which shall tide him over a few hours' delay wherever it may occur.

It is by no means a waste of time to familiarize ourselves with the geography at least of our own country; to know the situation and appearance of every city of importance, and to know something about the different railroads besides their initials, and their rating in the stock market. Again, if we take up the study of the trees, flowers and birds, with the aid of the admirable popular works now available, we shall not only view the scenery with new eyes, but shall welcome, rather than be driven to despair, by a breakdown in the woods.

It is a mistake to shun our fellow-travelers, from whom we should rather try to learn something. This is a solace in traveling alone, for the boon companion may handicap us in cultivating new acquaintances and gaining new impressions. Though the main object of recreation is diversion from the daily round of thought, the fact need not be lost sight of that the busy man will find his practical interests furthered, rather than hindered, by a little widening of the horizon. Nor should he forget, meantime, the admonition of Seneca that if he would wish his travels delightful he must first make himself delightful.

It is inevitable that uncomfortable, as well as agreeable, experiences occur in travel. But the man who spends his time and thought in avoiding the one and seeking the other is steadily forging chains whose gall shall one day surpass the discomforts of a journey around the world. Arthur Benson in "Beside Still Waters" says that Hugh learned one thing at school, namely, that the disagreeable was not necessarily the intolerable. Some of us would do well to go back to school and learn this over again. I know of only two ways by which the discomforts of travel can be avoided. One is to ignore them, the other to stay at home.

A fellow traveler told me that on one occasion, in the presence of a beautiful bit of mountain scenery, he overheard two ladies in anxious consultation comparing, article by article, the corresponding menus of two rival hotels. The fact that three varieties of fish were offered at one, while only two were offered at the other, opened so animated a discussion of quantity as opposed to probable quality that the listener discretely withdrew.

A lady on the Florida express, after reading a novel all day with an occasional interim, during which she gazed through her lorgnette with bored and anxious air, finally said to her companion, "I have not seen a single estate which compares to those in Brookline."

Among the varieties of needless worry imposed upon the traveler by the insistent habit, none is more common, or more easily overcome, than the refusal to sleep unless noise and light are quite shut out. If the sufferer make of his insistent habit a servant, rather than a master, and instead of reiterating "I must have quiet and darkness," will confidently assert, "I must get over this nonsense," he will speedily learn that freedom from resentment, and a good circulation of air, are more conducive to sleep than either darkness or silence.

The best drug for the sleepless traveler is the animo of Cicero.

XIII.

THE WORRIER AT THE TABLE

These little things are great to little man.

GOLDSMITH: The Traveller.

The insistent habit of mind is nowhere more noticeable than in connection with the food. I have seen a hotel, apparently sane, who invariably cut, or broke, his bread into minute particles, and minutely inspected each before placing it in his mouth. If this were a book of confessions, I should have myself to plead guilty, among worse things, to having avoided mince pie for weeks after encountering among other ingredients of this delicacy, a piece of broken glass.

Not infrequently the obsessive diner so long hesitates before giving his final order that the waiter brings the wrong dish. The insistent thought now replaces the doubting folly, and the diner would as soon think of eating grass as the article offered. I have known him impatiently to leave the table under these circumstances, and to play the ostentatious martyr, rather than partake of the food he had at the outset given weighty consideration. I have seen another omit his lunch because water had been spilled upon the cloth, and still another leave the dining-car, with the announcement that he would forego his meal because informed by the conductor that men's shirt waists without coats were taboo.

The obsessive of this type may by training even reach the point of seeing the amusing instead of the pathetic side of the picture when, in the course of his travels, his request for "a nice bit of chicken, cut thin," is transmitted to the kitchen as--"One chick."

One day, with pride, I called the attention of my easy-going friend to the fact that I was eating a dish I had not ordered. He quietly remarked that the next step was to eat it and say nothing! Another friend has this motto in his dining-room: "Eat what is set before you and be thankful." His children will open their eyes when they find others, less reasonably reared, demanding that the potatoes be changed because they are sprinkled with parsley, that a plate be replaced because it has had a piece of cheese upon it, or that the salad of lettuce and tomato be removed in favor of one with tomato alone.

A lady recently told me of breakfasting with a foreign sojourner in America, who upon being offered the contents of an egg broken into a glass, was not satisfied with declining it, but felt impelled also to express his extreme disgust at this method of serving it, fortunately to the amusement, rather than to the annoyance of his hostess.

"After this, know likewise," says Epictetus, "that you are a brother too; and that to this character it belongs to make concessions, to be easily persuaded, to use gentle language, never to claim for yourself any non-essential thing, but cheerfully to give up these to be repaid by a larger share of things essential. For consider what it is, instead of a lettuce, for instance, or a chair, to procure for yourself a good temper. How great an advantage gained!"

The insistent desire to have a certain degree and character of appetite not infrequently leads to consulting the physician. Still more common is the obsession that the appetite must be gratified, the supposition being that the desire for food is, in the growing child or in the adult, an infallible guide to the amount needed, though it is a matter of common knowledge that this is not true of infants or of domestic animals. If one leaves the table hungry he soon forgets it unless inordinately self-centered, and he has no more desire to return than to go back to bed and finish the nap so reluctantly discontinued in the morning.

I have heard the theory advanced by an anxious forecaster of future ills, that all unnecessary food, if packed away as adipose tissue, serves to nourish the body in periods of starvation. Assuming that the average individual need consider this stress of circumstance, I am strongly of the impression that the best preparation for enforced abstinence will prove, not a layer of fat, but the habit of abstinence. The nursery poet says:

"The worry cow would have lived till now If she'd only saved her breath. She feared the hay wouldn't last all day So choked herself to death."

The quantity of food proved by experiment to suffice for the best work, physical or mental, is surprisingly small. A feeling of emptiness, even, is better preparation for active exercise than one of satiety.

It is a national obsession with us that no meal is complete without meat. Order fruit, a cereal, rolls and coffee, at the hotel some morning, and the chances are ten to one that the waiter will ask what you are going to have for _breakfast_, though you have already ordered more than is absolutely necessary for that meal, as demonstrated by the custom upon the Continent, where the sense of fitness is as much violated by the consumption of an enormous breakfast as it is with us by the omission of a single detail.

It may be asked if it is not subversive of discipline for the hotel to become too easy-going. There is doubtless a limit to the virtue of allowing ourselves to be imposed upon, but there is little fear that the individual who opens the question will err in this direction. It behooves him rather to consider the danger of his occupying the unenviable position of the "fuss-budget."

XIV.

THE FEAR OF BECOMING INSANE

We must be steadfast, Julian! Satan is very busy in all of us.

IBSEN: Emperor and Galilean.

Few, perhaps, among the high-strung and delicately organized can truly say that this fear has never occurred to them. It affects even children, at an age when their minds are supposed to be taken up with the pleasures and pursuits appropriate to their years. This fear is generally dispelled by the serious occupations of life, but in certain cases it persists as an insistent and compelling thought.

It may afford consolation to know that insanity results, in the majority of cases, from physical disease of the brain, and that it is ordinarily unanticipated, unsuspected and uncredited by the patient. There is no more danger of insanity attacking the worrier and the delicate than the robust and the indifferent. In fact, the temperament which produces the faulty habits we are considering rarely culminates in insanity. It seems worth while, however, to replace the vague fear of insanity by a knowledge of the variety of mental unbalance remotely threatening the person who lacks the desire or the will, to place a check upon these faulty habits of mind. We may thus, in the worrier whose fears have taken this direction, substitute effort for foreboding.

It is our conduct rather than our thoughts that determines the question of insanity. The most practical definition of insanity I know is that of Spitzka, the gist of which is that a person is insane who can no longer correctly register impressions from the outside world, or can no longer act upon those impressions so as to formulate and carry out a line of conduct consistent with his age, education and station.

The banker may repeat the process of locking and unlocking, even to the point of doubting his own sensations, but he may still be able to formulate, and carry out, a line of conduct consistent with his position, though at the expense of intense mental suffering.

In the realm of morbid fears, the person obsessed by fear of contamination shows no sign of insanity in using tissue paper to turn the door-knob, or in avoiding objects that have been touched by others. Up to this point his phobia has led merely to eccentricity, but suppose his fear so far dominates him that he can no longer pursue his occupation for fear of handling tools or pen, and that he persistently refuses to eat through fear of poison, he has then reached the point where he can no longer formulate lines of conduct, and he is insane.

It is, then, important to foresee the tendency of phobias, and to accustom one's self to the point of view that the worst possible harm, for example from contamination by ordinary objects, is no worse than mental unbalance, and that the probable consequences thereof (_nil_) are infinitely preferable.

Even with regard to more tangible fears, as of elevators, fires, tunnels, thunder-storms, and the like, a certain tranquility may be gradually attained by a similar philosophy. Suppose instead of dwelling on the possibility of frightful disaster the sufferer practices saying: "The worst that can happen to me is no worse than for me to let these fears gradually lessen my sphere of operations till I finally shut myself up in my chamber and become a confirmed hypochondriac." One should also remember that many another shares his fears, but shows no sign because he keeps a "stiff upper lip," an example he will do well to follow, not only for his own eventual comfort, but for the sake of his influence on others, particularly on those younger than himself. The pursuance of this line of thought may result in the former c

of avoiding, opportunities to ride in elevators and tunnels, and even to occupy an inside seat at the theatre, just to try his new-found power, and to rejoice in doing as others do instead of being set apart as a hopeless crank.

These fears bear directly on the question of hypochondria. We have already seen how the sphere of the hypochondriac is narrowed. His work and his play are alike impeded by his fear of drafts, of wet feet, of loud noises, of palpitation, of exhaustion, of pain, and eventually of serious disease. Is he insane? Not so long as he can carry out a line of conduct consistent with his station and surroundings.

It is remarkable how many obsessions we may harbor without causing us to swerve from our accustomed line of conduct. Whatever our thoughts, our conduct may be such that we attract little attention beyond the passing observation that we are a little odd. We may break down, it is true, under the double load we carry, but we are in little danger of insanity. Those established in the conviction that they cannot stand noises or other sources of discomfort, rarely reach the point of a certain poor old lady who used to wander from clinic to clinic, able to think of nothing else, and to talk of nothing else, than the ringing in her ears, and to attend to no other business than efforts for its relief. She was counselled again and again that since nothing was to be found in the ears she should endeavor to reconcile herself to the inevitable, and turn her thoughts in other directions. Unfortunately, she had become peculiarly adept in the detection of disagreeable sights, sounds, and other sources of irritation, and had for a long term of years practiced quite the opposite of control. She had hitherto either insisted on discontinuance of all sources of irritation, fled their neighborhood, or put on blue glasses and stopped her ears with cotton. When, finally, her sharpened sense caught the sound of her own circulation, she could think of nothing but this unavoidable source of discomfort, which was prepared to follow her to the uttermost parts of the earth.

A well-known author has said that the difference between sanity and insanity depends only on the power to conceal the emotions. While this definition will hardly pass in law or medicine, it surely offers food for thought. Suppose for a moment that we were dominated by the impulse to externalize all our thoughts and all our emotions, there would be some basis for the common, but inaccurate, saying that everyone is insane.

This brings us to a form of insanity which the obsessive may well bear in mind, namely, that known as manic-depressive. This disorder, in its typical form, is shown by recurring outbursts of uncontrollable mental and physical activity (mania), alternating with attacks of profound depression (melancholia). This form of insanity represents the inability to control an extreme degree of the varied moods to which we all are subject. Long before the modern classification of mental disorders, Burton, in his introduction to the "Anatomy of Melancholy," expressed this alternation of moods thus:

"When I go musing all alone, Thinking of divers things foreknown, When I build castles in the ayr, Void of sorrow and void of feare, Pleasing myself with phantasms sweet, Me thinks the time runs very fleet. All my joyes to this are folly, Naught so sweet as melancholy.

"When I lie waking all alone, Recounting what I have ill done, My thoughts on me they tyrannize, Feare and sorrow me surprise, Whether I tarry still or go, Me thinks the time moves very slow. All my griefs to this are jolly, Naught so sad as melancholy."

* * * * *

"I'll not change my life with any King, I ravisht am: can the world bring More joy, than still to laugh and smile, In pleasant toyes time to beguile? Do not, O do not trouble me, So sweet content I feel and see. All my joyes to this are folly, None so divine as melancholy.

"I'll change my state with any wretch Thou canst from goale or dunghill fetch: My pain's past cure, another hell, I may not in this torment dwell, Now desperate I hate my life, Lend me a halter or a knife; All my griefs to this are jolly, None so damn'd as melancholy."

The depressed stage of this disorder is commonly shown by retardation of thought and motion, the excited stage by pressure of activity and acceleration of thought. In the so-called "flight of ideas" words succeed each other with incredible rapidity, without goal idea, but each word suggesting the next by sound or other association, thus:

"Are you blue?"

"Blue, true blue, red white and blue, one flag and one nation, one kingdom, one king, no not one king, one president, we are going to have a president first, cursed, the worst."

Who does not recognize the modest prototype of this elaborate rigmarole chasing itself through his mind as he walks the street in jaunty mood, and who of us would not surprise and alarm his friends if he should suddenly let go his habitual control, express his every thought and materialize his every passing impulse to action? Who can doubt that the person who has trained himself for years to repress his obsessions is less likely to give way to this form of insanity than one who has never practiced such training? Let us then endeavor to pursue "the even tenor of our way" without giving way to the obsession that we must inflict our feelings upon our associates. We may in this way maintain a mental balance that shall stand us in good stead in time of stress.

The autumnal tendency to melancholy is recognized by Thoreau. The characteristic suggestion of this nature-lover is that the melancholic go to the woods and study the symplocarpus foetidus (skunk cabbage), whose English name savors of contempt, but whose courage is such that it is already in the autumn jauntily thrusting forth its buds for the coming year.

An admirable reflection for the victim of moods, as for many another, is the old saying in which Abraham Lincoln is said to have taken peculiar comfort, namely, "This also will pass."

XV.

RECAPITULATORY

And found no end in wandering mazes lost.

Paradise Lost.

We have reviewed the various phases of worry and the elements out of which worry is assembled. It has been seen that exaggerated self-consciousness blocks effort through fear of criticism, ridicule or comment. The insistent habit of mind in the worrier has been found to permeate the content of thought, and unfavorably to influence action. The fact has been pointed out that the obsession to do the right thing may be carried so far as to produce querulous doubt and chronic indecision--hence worry.

It has been pointed out that over-anxiety on the score of health (hypochondria) aggravates existing symptoms, and itself develops symptoms; that these symptoms in turn increase the solicitude which gave them birth. Attention has been called to the influence of over-anxious and fretful days in precluding the restful state of mind that favors sleep, and to the influence of the loss of sleep upon the anxieties of the following day; in other words, worry prevents sleep, and inability to sleep adds to worry.

We have seen that doubts of fitness lead to unfitness, and that the worry of such doubts, combined with futile regrets for the past and forebodings for the future, hamper the mind which should be cleared for present action.

The injurious effect upon the nervous system of these faulty mental states has been emphasized, together with their influence as potent underlying causes of so-called nervous prostration, preparing the worrier for breakdown from an amount of work which, if undertaken with tranquil mind, could have been accomplished with comparative ease.

The question is, will the possessor of these faulty mental tendencies grasp the importance of giving thought to the training that shall free him from the incubus? He certainly has the intelligence, for it is among the intelligent that these states are mostly found; he certainly has the will-power, for lack of will-power is not a failing of the obsessed. The question is, can he bring himself to make, at the suggestion of another, a fundamental change of attitude, and will he take these suggestions on faith, though many seem trivial, others, perhaps, unreasonable, and will he at least give them a trial? I hope so.

In the next sections will be summed up such commonplace and simple suggestions as may aid emergence from the maze of worry. Many of the suggestions have been scattered through preceding sections. The worrier and folly-doubter is more likely to be benefited by trying them than by arguing about them, and it is within the realms of possibility that some may come to realize the truth of the paradox that he who loses himself shall find himself.

XVI.

MAXIMS MISAPPLIED

"Beware! yet once again beware! Ere round thy inexperienced mind, With voice and semblance falsely fair, A chain Thessalian magic bind,--"

Thomas Love Peacock.

A friend of mine has a highbred Boston terrier named "Betty." Betty is a bundle of nerves, has a well-developed "New-England Conscience," and among other deviative (not degenerative) signs is possessed of an insatiate desire to climb trees. More than once I have watched her frantic efforts to achieve this end, and she really almost succeeds--at least she can reach a higher point on the trunk of a tree than any other dog of her size I know--say six feet; if the bark is rough, perhaps seven feet would not be an overestimate. Her attempts are unremitting--once the frenzy is on it is with the greatest difficulty that she can be separated, panting and exhausted, from her task.

Betty's case furnishes an illustration of an inborn tendency, fostered neither by precept nor example, persistently to attempt the impossible, and to fret and fume when forced to discontinue. Some children are by inheritance similarly endowed. Imagine Betty a child. It is safe to assume that the mental trait which prompts this expenditure of tireless and misdirected energy has sifted down through her ancestry; the chances are, of course, against its having skipped the generation immediately preceding; in other words, one or both her parents are probably obsessive. It follows almost as a matter of course that the "indomitable will" of the child is viewed with pride by the parent. Instead of being kept within reasonable bounds, and directed into proper channels, it is encouraged in every direction, and fostered by every available means. Prominent among the incentives to renewed activity furnished by the solicitous parent, possibly by the undiscriminating teacher, will be found such precepts as: "In the bright lexicon of youth there's no such word as fail," "Never give up the ship," "Never say die," "There's always room at the top."

Excellent maxims these, for the average child, particularly for the child who is under average as regards ambition to excel. But what of their effect upon the already over-conscientious and self-exacting child? Simply to tighten fetters which should rather be relaxed.

Life becomes a serious problem to a child of this kind at a much earlier age than is generally realized. I have been surprised to learn at what tender years such children have been borne down by a weight of self-imposed responsibility quite as heavy as can burden an adult, without the power of the adult to carry it. Such, for example, are anxieties regarding the health or the financial status of the parents, matters freely discussed without a thought that the child will make these cares his own.

I realize that this line of thought will seem to some revolutionary. A friend to whom I submitted the proposition that it did harm rather than good to encourage a child of this kind to attempt the impossible answered, "Nothing is impossible," and he said it as if he more than half believed it. Here we have the ambitious maxim challenging truth itself. It is certainly not impossible that Mozart wrote a difficult concerto at the age of five; nor is it impossible that, in precocious children of a different type, worry from failure to accomplish the desired may cause profound despair productive of disastrous results.

Nor are such children either geniuses or freaks--they are merely inheritors of the "New England Conscience," so named, I suppose, because the trait has multiplied in this section more rapidly even than the furniture and fittings of the Mayflower. Without underrating the sterling qualities of the devoted band who founded this community it may safely be suggested that neither the effectiveness nor the staying qualities of their descendants will be lessened by a certain modification of the querulous insistence which dominates the overtrained adult in the rearing of the nervously precocious child.

The maxim "What is worth doing at all is worth doing well," if carried to its ultimate conclusion by the over-careful, would justify the expenditure of a quarter of an hour in sharpening a lead-pencil. This maxim, while losing in sententiousness would gain in reason if it ran thus: "What is worth doing at all is worth doing as well as the situation demands." "Never put off till to-morrow what you can do to-day," an excellent maxim for the shiftless, must not be taken too literally by the individual already obsessed to do to-day twice what he can and quadruple what he ought.

Neither the chronic doubter nor the prematurely thoughtful need be admonished, "Look before you leap," or "Be sure you're right, then go ahead." Such guides to conduct, however effective in the case of three individuals, in the fourth hinder accomplishment by encouraging querulous doubt;--it is for the benefit of the fourth that these pages are written. A revolutionary effort must be made before the worrier and the folly-doubter can throw off his shackles.

It may be questioned whether this sort of philosophy does not savor of _laissez-faire_, and tend to produce indifference; but the worry against which these efforts are directed is a state of undue solicitude,--due solicitude is not discouraged. Fortunately, as partial offset to the many maxims stirring to increased activity, there exist certain maxims of less strenuous, but not unreasonable, trend, thus:--"What can't be cured must be endured," "Patient waiters are no losers." Such maxims are quite as worthy of consideration by the obsessive as any of those previously cited. While they modify overzeal, they detract in no way from effective, even strenuous, endeavor.

XVII.

THE FAD

"Fads may be said to constitute a perfect mental antitoxin for the poison generated by cerebral acuity."

Courtney.

There is nothing occult in the suggestion that the worrier cultivate a fad. Its object is to interest him in something outside of himself and of the monotony of his accustomed round. If it seems to him too much trouble to enter upon the details of the fad there is all the more reason for freeing himself from such mental inertia.

How shall we set to work to acquire a fad, without special opportunity or education, and with but little time at our disposal? Suppose we take the study of botany as an illustration, not necessitating class instruction. This useful study may be made also a charming fad, and one not beneath the notice of so learned and busy a man as Sir Francis Bacon, who found time and inclination to write an essay "Of Gardens," in which he mentions by name and shows intimate acquaintance with, over one hundred distinct varieties of plant life.

Sir John Lubbock (the Right Honourable Lord Avebury) in "The Pleasures of Life," says:

"The botanist, on the contrary--nay, I will not say the botanist, but one with even a slight knowledge of that delightful science--when he goes out into the woods, or out into one of those fairy forests which we call fields, finds himself welcomed by a glad company of friends, every one with something interesting to tell."

There are two ways of cultivating botanical as well as other knowledge; namely, the passive and the active. The passive method is to let someone inform us; the active is to find out something for ourselves. The latter is the only effective method. Suppose we start with the wild flowers:

The first step is to purchase a popular illustrated book on this subject, preferably one in which the flowers are arranged according to color. We first learn, in the introduction, the principal parts of the flower, as the calyx, the corolla, the stamen and the pistil. We find that the arrangements of leaves and flowers are quite constant, that the leaves of some plants are opposite, of others alternate; of still others from the root only, that flowers are solitary, in raceme, head, spike or otherwise clustered.

It now behooves us to take a walk upon a country road with our eyes open and our book under our arm. Along the roadsides passing vehicles have scattered the seeds of many flowering plants. We decide to pick and learn the first white blossom we see. This blossom appears, we will say, upon a plant about a foot high. We notice that its leaves are opposite, that its corolla has five petals and that its calyx is inflated. We now look through the section on white flowers. The first plant described has leaves from the root only; the second is a tall shrub, these we pass, therefore, and continue until we find one answering the description, leaves opposite, calyx inflated, corolla of five petals. When we reach it we have identified the plant; we now feel a sense of ownership in the _Bladder Campion_, and are quite shocked when our friend calls it only "a weed." Meantime we have noted many familiar names and some familiar illustrations which we must identify on our next ramble.

On consulting our timepiece we find that we have absolutely spent a couple of hours in complete forgetfulness of the daily grind, to say nothing of having filled our lungs with comparatively fresh air, and having taken a little exercise. Best of all, we have started a new set of associations; we have paved the way for new acquaintances, Linnaeus, Gray, Dioscorides and Theophrastus, to say nothing of our friend _so-and-so_ whom we always thought rather tiresome but with whom we now have something in common. We shall take up our daily grind to-morrow with a new zest for having forgotten it for a few hours, and find it less of a grind than usual; moreover, we now have an object to encourage another stroll in the country.

If we continue as we have begun we shall soon find ourselves prying into the more scientific works on botany, and perhaps eventually extending our interest to the birds, the beasts and the boulders. One of these days we may become quite proficient amateur naturalists, but this is only by the way; the real advantage to us has been the externalizing of our interests.

This is the most desultory way possible of cultivating the fad. One may go a step further and transplant the wild flowers and the weeds. A busy and successful professional friend of mine, besides having a cabinet shop in his stable, finds (or makes) time to go to the woods with his trowel. He has quite a wild-flower bank in his garden. I cannot give definite directions as to their setting out--I think he just throws them down anywhere--a fair percentage seem to thrive,--I can remember the larger bur-marigold, the red and white bane-berry, rattlesnake-weed, rattlesnake-plantain, blood root, live-for-ever, wood betony, pale corydalis, and fern-leaved foxglove, and there are many more.

Mushrooms and ferns offer fertile fields for special study. If the worrier has an altruistic turn he will find satisfaction in bestowing duplicates upon his friends, thus still further externalizing his interests. He will be surprised to find how many things there are in the world that he never noticed.

Whether our tastes lead us in the direction of photography, pottery, mechanics, collecting china, books and old furniture, of philosophy or a foreign language, we need not aim to pursue these avocations too profoundly. We must not compare our acquisitions with those of the savant or the skilled laborer, but must console ourselves with the reflection that we at least know more, or can do more, than yesterday. If our fads, now and then, make us do something that gives us a little trouble, so much the better, if it is only to go to the library for a book,--the worrier whose idea of rest and recuperation is to remain forever glued to an easy-chair is indeed to be pitied.

Collecting old prints, stamps, and coins, is by no means a waste of time. Fads of this nature offer the additional inducement of an asset which may serve, in a material way, to banish worry in time of stress. To reap the full advantage of the collection fads one should take pains to acquire a knowledge of the geography and history with which they are associated. Few are so unfortunately placed that they have no access to information on these subjects. The encyclop鋘ia, at least, is within general reach, though rarely consulted by those who most need its aid.

Suppose one takes up history for an indoor fad. How shall he start in? Since he pursues this study only as a fad, he can commence almost anywhere. Let him decide to become familiar with the fifteenth century. The first step is to familiarize himself with the principal rulers and the principal battles of that time. Suppose he spends half an hour every evening upon the life of one or another ruler, as given in the encyclopedia or elsewhere. If he is sufficiently inventive to construct a pictorial or other plan in which to give each his place, so much the better. Having thus constructed a framework he can begin to fill in the details, and now the study begins to interest him. At any public library he can find a catalogue of historical fiction arranged according to centuries. Under the fifteenth century he will find Quentin Durward, The Broad Arrow, Anne of Geierstein, The Cloister and the Hearth, Every Inch a King, Marietta, The Dove in the Eagle's Nest, and other standard works, all of which he may have read before, but every page of which will have for him a new interest since he can now place the characters, appreciate the customs, and form a consistent picture of what was doing in different countries at this time.

The next step is to acquire, in the same way, equal familiarity with the preceding and succeeding centuries, particularly with the interrelations of the different countries, old and new.

The reader who has followed to this point will need no further hint. If he continues as he has begun, he will be surprised to find how soon he will be able to instruct, on one subject at least, the college graduate, unless that graduate has happily continued as a fad what he once perfunctorily acquired.

Another way of commencing this study, and the one, I confess, which appeals more to me, is first to establish a framework which shall cover a long period of time, then study special epochs. An interesting way to start this method is to purchase Creasy's "Decisive Battles of the World," and familiarize one's self with its contents. This will furnish pegs on which to hang further items of information, and will impart a running familiarity with different nations involved in war from the time of the supremacy of Greece, down to the battle of Manila, in the recent edition,--in earlier editions to the time of Napoleon.

The only absolutely essential reference book for this study is Ploetz's "Epitome of Universal History."

To make this fad interesting, the mere commitment to memory of facts and dates will not suffice. Items of history thus acquired will inevitably fade. The conscientious but ill-advised student who attempts to commit the "Epitome" to memory will fall by the way-side. Time is not wasted in dwelling sufficiently long on one subject to feel a sense of ownership in it, and there is opportunity for the exercise of individual ingenuity in devising means to accomplish this end. If one has the knack, for example, of writing nonsense verse (and this is a talent all too easy of cultivation) it will aid him in fixing by rhyme names and dates otherwise difficult to master, thus:

"Ten sixty-six is a date you must fix;" or "Drake was not late in fifteen eighty-eight."

The study of music, history, trees, flowers, or birds doubtless seems of trivial interest to one who occupies his leisure hours with such weighty problems as figuring out how rich he would have been to-day if he had bought Bell Telephone at 15, but such study is far more restful, and in the long run quite as useful for the over-busy man.

It is not necessary to devote an enormous amount of time to such pursuits. One has only to purchase Miss Huntington's "Studies of Trees in Winter" and learn the trees in his own doorway, or upon his street, to awaken an interest that will serve him in good stead upon a railroad journey, or during an otherwise monotonous sojourn in the country. A walk around the block before dinner with such an object in view is more restful than pondering in one's easy-chair over the fluctuations of the stock market, and the man who is "too busy" for such mental relaxation is paving the way for ultimate, perhaps early, breakdown.

Once started on the trees, the man who did not even know that their buds were visible in the winter, after absorbing the contents of the popular tree-books may find himself looking for something more elaborate. He may even look forward to his next western trip with pleasure instead of disgust, now that he anticipates seeing at close hand the eucalyptus, the Monterey cypress, and the pinus ponderosa.

Courtney says "to all this will undoubtedly be objected the plea of lack of time. The answer to arguments formed on such flimsy basis is that all the time which is spent in preparing one's self as a candidate for a sanitarium is like the proverbial edged tool in the hands of children and fools."

A little time spent in such simple pursuits as I have indicated, and a few weeks' vacation _before exhaustion appears_, may prevent a year's enforced abstinence from work on account of nervous invalidism. I am tempted here to say "A stitch in time saves nine," but adages are sometimes dangerous. Thus the adage, "If you want a thing well done you must do it yourself," has caused many a business and professional man to burden himself with details which in the long run he might better have intrusted to subordinates, even at the risk of an occasional blunder.

It is not wise to specialize too much in the pursuit of the fad. Suppose the busy man, having conceded the value of some out-of-door study, decides that he will learn the lumber industry, but take no interest in the shade trees. He will not materially broaden his interests in this way. He will rather add to his burdens another business. If he applies to this new business the same conscientious methods which are wearing him out in his present one, the value of the fad is gone, the new study has done him more harm than good, and when on his vacation, unless there is a sawmill in the neighborhood, he finds himself stranded with only worry for company. Similarly, if the study of history is taken up in the way a fad should be taken up, anything in the way of a book will now interest the worrier, for hardly a book worth reading fails to contain either a bit of travel, geography, biography, law, or something on manners and customs.

Permanent freedom from worry involves a change in one's whole view of life and method of thought. But the means by which introspection may be temporarily alleviated are by no means to be despised. Among these comes the pursuit of the golf-ball. Many a business and professional man who thinks he has no time for golf can easily escape for an hour's play at the end of the day, twice a week, and in the long run it will prove to be time well expended. In point of fact, most are hindered rather by the notion that it is not worth while to visit the links unless one can play eighteen holes, or that it is not worth while to take up the game at all unless one can excel. But the exercise is the same, and the air equally bracing whether we win or lose; the shower-bath will refresh us just the same whether we have played nine holes or twenty-seven.

The automobile ride, the drive, and, best of all, the ride on horseback, will often serve to banish the vapors. Many neglect these methods, not from lack of time or money, but from indisposition.

A busy professional man recently assured me that he had renewed his youth by going three times a week to the gymnasium and joining the "old man's class." Here is an opportunity open to practically everyone; it is a desirable practice if continued. The drawback is the lack of incentive when the novelty has passed. Such incentive is furnished by the fad, in the satisfaction of gaining new knowledge and broadening the thought-associations.

XVIII.

HOME TREATMENT

Submit to what is unavoidable, banish the impossible from the mind, and look around for some new object of interest in life.

Goethe.

In the treatment of faulty mental habits the chief reliance is the training of the mind; physical measures are merely supplementary. This fact has always been recognized in a general way. The need of such training was emphasized by Epictetus thus:

"Not to be disappointed of our desire, nor incur our aversion. To this ought our training be directed. For without vigorous and steady training, it is not possible to preserve our desire undisappointed and our aversion unincurred."

But there has always been an undercurrent of dissatisfaction with purely mental treatment, and a desire for the drug, which has more than once, doubtless, been prescribed for the purpose of "suggestion" only.

The movement for psychic treatment on scientific principles, of faulty mental disorders, not of organic nature, is well under way. That the American profession takes an active interest in this movement is shown by the exhaustive paper on psycho-therapy by Dr. E. W. Taylor, recently read at a combined meeting held in Boston and discussed by such representative neurologists as Drs. Mills, Dercum, J. K. Mitchell, and Sinkler, of Philadelphia; Drs. Dana, Sachs, Collins, Hunt, Meacham, and Jelliffe, of New York; Dr. White of Washington, and Drs. Putnam and Prince, of Boston.

Such faulty mental habits as worry and obsession, doubting folly, and hypochondria, are no more amenable to physical treatment than the habit of swearing, or of over-indulgence in food and drink. Even the psychic treatment, by another, of such disorders, as of such habits, labors under the disadvantage that all attempts to influence another by exhortation, ridicule, or reproach are met by active or passive resistance on the part of the individual toward whom these efforts are directed. A conscientious resolve on the part of the individual himself, whether started by a casual hint or by a new line of thought, is often more effective than any amount of outside pressure, however well directed.

It is my hope and belief that the over-solicitous individual will be influenced by reading these descriptions to adopt, of his own initiative, some of these suggestions. His most striking peculiarity is his conviction that he cannot take the chances others do, that the criticisms he receives are peculiarly annoying, and that his sources of worry are something set apart from the experience of ordinary mortals. This conviction leads him to meet argument by argument, reproach and ridicule by indignant protest or brooding silence. The perusal of these sections may lead him to alter his ideals. Suggestions for home treatment have been scattered through the various pages; it only remains to sum them up.

We have traced worry back to exaggerated self-consciousness and obsession; it is against these two faulty tendencies that training may be directed.

The first step is the initiation of a new attitude, namely, the commonplace. The establishment of this attitude involves the sacrifice of self-love, and of the melancholy pleasure of playing the martyr. The oversensitive individual must recognize the fact that if people do not want him round it may be because he inflicts his ego too obtrusively upon his associates. He must realize that others are more interested in their own affairs than in his, and that however cutting their comments and unjust their criticisms, and however deeply these may sink into his soul, they are only passing incidents with them.

He must realize that if two people whisper they are not necessarily whispering about him, and if they are it is of no consequence, and merely shows their lack of breeding. On public occasions he must remember that others are thinking of themselves, or of the subject in hand, quite as much as they are of him and how he behaves. He must realize that even if he does something foolish it will only make a passing impression on others, and that they will like him none the less for it.

He must practice externalizing his thoughts. If criticised, he must ask himself whether the criticism is just or unjust. If just, he must learn to accept and act upon it; if unjust, he must learn to classify the critic, as unreasonable, thoughtless, or ill-natured, place him in the appropriate mental compartment, throw the criticism into the intellectual waste-basket, and proceed upon his way. This practice, difficult at first, will, if assiduously cultivated, become more and more automatic, and will materially modify a fruitful source of worry.

The next step is to practice the control of the dominating impulses (obsessions). If one finds himself impelled continually to drum, or walk the floor, he will find the habit cannot be dropped at once, but if he can refrain from it for a few moments once or twice in the day, no matter how lost he feels without it, and sit for a few minutes relaxed and motionless, the intervals can be gradually increased. Even the chronic doubter may appreciate the fact that this practice aids in preparing one for taking and keeping, at night, the quiet and immobile position which favors sleep. The bearing of this training upon worry may not be immediately obvious, but if one cannot overcome these simple physical compulsions he will find it still harder to overcome the doubts, the fears, and the scruples which underlie his worry.

It is hard to give up the idea that we are so peculiarly constituted that it produces a special disgust in our case if another constantly clears his throat, and a peculiar annoyance if he rocks. It is difficult to relinquish the belief that, however callous others may be, our nervous system is so delicately adjusted that we cannot work when others make unnecessary noise, and we cannot sleep if a clock ticks in our hearing. But if one persistently cultivates the commonplace, he will at last find himself seeking instead of avoiding the objects of his former torture, merely to exercise his new-found mastery of himself, and to realize that "He that ruleth his spirit is better than he that taketh a city."

It is the imperative duty of every sufferer from doubting folly to say to himself, "I will perform this act once with my whole attention, then leave it and turn my mind in other channels before I have dulled my perception by repetition."

If one is prone to chronic indecision, he must remind himself that it is better to do the wrong thing with single mind, than to work himself into a frenzy of anxious doubt. In case the choice is not an important one, he must learn to pounce upon either task, and waste no further time. If the doubt concerns an important matter, he must learn to devote only that attention to the matter which is commensurate with its importance, then decide it one way or the other, realizing that it is better to make a mistake, even in an important matter than to worry one's self into utter helplessness by conflicting emotions.

If insistent fear attacks one, he must remind himself that the worst that can happen to him is not so bad as the state of the chronic coward and the hypochondriac. He must practice taking the chances that others do, and must learn to go through the dreaded experiences, not with his nervous system stimulated into undue tension, but with body and mind relaxed by such considerations as I have indicated.

The maxim is a useful aid in suggestion, but it should be carefully selected. Most children seem to be brought up on maxims which presuppose mental deficiency and constitutional carelessness. But the naturally over-thoughtful and too-conscientious child, the child to whom applies Sir John Lubbock's observation that the term "happy childhood" is sometimes a misnomer, needs no admonition to "Try, try again," and to "Never weary of well doing."

Among other sayings, whether of home manufacture or acquired, I have often found comfort in a suggestion first called to my attention by my friend, Dr. Maurice Richardson, who carries, I believe, Epictetus in his bag, but who does not despise the lesser prophets. One day when I was borrowing trouble about some prospective calamity, he said he always drew consolation from the old farmer's observation:

"Mebbe 'taint so!"

Much unintentional self-suggestion is conveyed in one's habitual method of expressing his attitude toward annoyances, thus: "That simply drives me wild." Suppose, now, one should try a little substitution; for example:

That \ drives me wild. Nothing /

(but that). I can stand anything (at all).

(not) (this) I can sleep in position. (---) (any)

The quieting effect is immediately perceptible.

Nor is the injurious effect of the explosive habit of speech limited to the person who indulges it. The other day a lady, apparently in no haste, sauntered into a station of the "Elevated" ahead of me, holding by the hand a small boy. The boy was enjoying himself immensely, gazing about him with the wide-awake, but calmly contemplative air peculiar to childhood. Suddenly the lady saw that a train was about to leave the station, and was seized by the not uncommon compulsion to take the last train instead of the next one. She hurried the boy across the platform only to meet the closed door of the departing train.

"_Isn't_ that _provoking_!" she exclaimed. And the boy began to whimper.

Although the main object of this book is to call attention to the mental rather than the physical treatment of these states, I cannot forbear reminding the reader of certain routine measures which facilitate the desired improvement in mental attitude.

It is well to start the day with a quick plunge in cold water, that is, in water of the natural temperature excepting in the cold season, when the extreme chill may be taken off to advantage. A brisk rub with rough towels should follow. One should proceed immediately from the warm bed to the bath, and should not first "cool off." A few setting-up exercises (bending the trunk forward and back, sidewise, and with a twist) may precede the bath, and a few simple arm exercises follow it. A few deep breaths will inevitably accompany these procedures. When one returns to his room he no longer notices the chill in the air, and he has made a start toward accustoming himself to, and really enjoying, lower temperatures than he fancied he could stand at all.

Every healthy adult should walk at least two miles daily in the open. We have been forced to readjust our ideas as to the distance even an elderly person can walk without harm since a pedestrian of sixty-nine has, without apparent injury, covered over one thousand miles, over ordinary roads, at an average of fifty miles a day.

The day's work should be started with the resolution that every task shall be taken up in its turn, without doubts and without forebodings, that bridges shall not be crossed until they are reached, that the vagaries of others shall amuse and interest, not distress us, and that we will live in the present, not in the past or the future. We must avoid undertaking too much, and whatever we do undertake we must try not to worry as to whether we shall succeed. This only prevents our succeeding. We should devote all our efforts to the task itself, and remember that even failure under these circumstances may be better than success at the expense of prolonged nervous agitation.

"Rest must be complete when taken and must balance the effort in work--rest meaning often some form of recreation as well as the passive rest of sleep. Economy of effort should be gained through normal concentration--that is, the power of erasing all previous impressions and allowing a subject to hold and carry us, by dropping every thought or effort that interferes with it, in muscle, nerve, and mind." (Annie Payson Call, "Power Through Repose.")

The over-scrupulous and methodical individual who can neither sleep nor take a vacation until all the affairs of his life are arranged must remind himself that this happy consummation will not be attained in his lifetime. It behooves him, therefore, if he is ever to sleep, or if he is ever to take a vacation, to do it now, nor need he postpone indefinitely

"That blessed mood In which the burden of the mystery, In which the heavy and the weary weight Of all this unintelligible world Is lightened."

XIX.

HOME TREATMENT (CONTINUED)

Happiness and success in life do not depend on circumstances, but on ourselves.

Sir John Lubbock.

The obsession to "arrive" is a fertile source of fret and worry. This habit of mind leads to frantic and impatient labor and blocks our pleasure at every point. The person who plays a game only to see who wins loses half the benefit of the recreation. Here are two ways of walking the half-mile to and from my office:

Suppose I start out with my mind on my destination, thinking only of what I shall do when I get there, and how I shall do it. This thought influences my whole body. I am all "keyed up," my muscles are tense, my breathing, even, is constricted and the walk does me comparatively little good.

Suppose, now, I decide I am making a mistake, and determine to live in the present. General relaxation follows, I take a deep breath, and begin to notice my surroundings. I may even observe the sky-line of the buildings I have passed daily for years without knowing they had a sky-line; my gait becomes free and life takes on a different aspect. I have taken a long step toward mental tranquility as well as gaining "power through repose."

One of the hardest obsessions to overcome is the unduly insistent habit of mind regarding orderliness and cleanliness. It is not undue to desire and practice a reasonable degree of these virtues, but when it gives one a "fit" to see a picture slightly off the level, and drives one "wild" to see a speck of dust, it is time to modify the ideal. This is the frame of mind which encourages worry over trifles. If one really wishes to lessen worry he must cultivate a certain degree of tolerance for what does not square with his ideas, even if it does violence to a pet virtue.

The careful housekeeper may object that so long as she can regulate her household to her liking, the habit of orderliness, even though extreme, causes her no worry. But it is only the hermit housekeeper who can entirely control her household. And further, the possessor of the over-orderly temperament, whether applied to housekeeping, business, or play (if he ever plays), is bound sooner or later to impinge his ideas of orderliness upon the domain of other peoples' affairs, in which his wishes cannot be paramount. In this event, at least, he will experience a worry only to be allayed by learning to stand something he does not like.

Worry about the mental condition is disastrous. The habit should be cultivated of taking the mind for what it is, and using it, wasting no time in vain regrets that it is not nimbler or more profound. Just as the digestion is impeded by solicitude, so the working of the brain is hampered by using the energy in worry which should be devoted directly to the task in hand. Children frequently worry because their memory is poor. It should be explained to them that in ninety-nine cases out of a hundred apparent lack of memory is only lack of attention, and they should be urged to cease distracting the attention by wandering in the fields of idle speculation or in making frantic leaps to surmount imaginary obstacles.

It is important for parents of morbidly sensitive and over-scrupulous children, with acute likes and dislikes, to discourage the tendency of the child to become more and more peculiar. Sensitive children are inclined to worry because they think others do not care for them or want them round. If such children can be led to take a bird's-eye view of themselves, they may be made to realize that others crave their society according as they are helpful, entertaining, sympathetic, or tactful, because they instil courage and give comfort. They should be urged, therefore, to cultivate these qualities instead of wasting their energy in tears and recriminations; and they should be encouraged to practice such of these traits as they can master instead of becoming moody in society, or withdrawing to brood in solitude, either of which errors may result in producing on the part of others a genuine dislike. In other words, teach them to avoid enforcing too far their ego on themselves or their environment.

Parents must also remember that over-solicitous attention on their part is bound to react to the disadvantage of the child. The story is told of Phillips Brooks that, when a child, he put a newly sharpened pencil into his mouth further and further until it slipped down his throat. He asked his mother what would happen if anyone should swallow a pencil. She answered that she supposed it would kill him. Phillips kept silence, and his mother made no further inquiry.

This incident would indicate that Phillips Brooks had already, as a child, attained a mental equipoise which the average individual hardly achieves in a lifetime. The story appeals to me no less as evidence of self-control on the part of the mother; and I like to imagine that she suppressed the question a startled parent naturally would ask, realizing that no amount of worry would recall the pencil if he had swallowed it, and that nothing was to be gained by overturning the household, or by giving the boy an example of agitation sure to react to the detriment of the mind unfolding under her supervision. Unless, therefore, the facts of this story have become distorted by imagery, it shows exceptional heredity and unusual training.

Not every one can claim such heredity, and not every one can look back on such training; but it is not too much to say that every one can so direct his thoughts and so order his actions as gradually to attain a somewhat higher level of self-control than either his mental endowment or his early training would have promised. For mental training is no more limited to feats of memory, and to practice in the solution of difficult problems, than is physical training comprised in the lifting of heavy weights in harness. In fact, such exercises are always in danger of leaving the mental athlete intellectually muscle-bound, if I may use such an expression; whereas the kind of training I have in mind tends to establish mental poise, to improve the disposition, to fit the mind (and indirectly the body) better to meet the varied exigencies of daily life, and to help the individual to react in every way more comfortably to his surroundings.

I have only hinted at the detailed suggestions by which the worry habit and allied faulty mental tendencies may be combated. The obsessive who is able to alter his ideals and systematically pursue the line of thought here sketched will himself find other directions in which control can be exercised. It is true that no one is likely to reach any of the extreme degrees of incapacity we have considered unless he is naturally endowed with a mind predestined to unbalance. At the same time any of us who have a nervous temperament ever so slightly above the average of intensity will do well to check these tendencies as far as possible in their incipiency, realizing that no physical evil we may dread can be worse than the lot of the confirmed hypochondriac or the compulsively insane.

Perhaps I have dwelt too much upon the extreme results of morbid mental tendencies, and too little upon the ideal for which we should strive. This ideal I shall not attempt to portray, but leave it rather to the imagination. Suffice it to say that the ladder by which self-control is attained is so long that there is ample room to ascend and descend without reaching either end. Some of us are started high on the ladder, some low; but it is certainly within the power of each to alter somewhat his level. We can slide down, but must climb up; and that such commonplaces as are here presented may help some of my fellow worriers to gain a rung or two is my earnest wish. Even when we slip back we can appreciate the sentiment of Ironsides:

"Night after night the cards were fairly shuffled And fairly dealt, but still I got no hand. The morning came, but I with mind unruffled Did simply say, 'I do not understand.'

"Life is a game of whist; from unseen sources The cards are shuffled and the hands are dealt. Vain are our efforts to control the forces, Which, though unseen, are no less strongly felt.

"I do not like the way the cards are shuffled, But still I like the game and want to play, And through the long, long night with mind unruffled, Play what I get until the dawn of day."

###

www.ingramcontent.com/pod-product-compliance
Lightning Source LLC
Chambersburg PA
CBHW071059290526
45795CB00004B/1569